P9-DXM-791

SUMMIT

English for Today's World

1

Joan Saslow • Allen Ascher

Pronunciation Booster by Bertha Chela-Flores

PEARSON
Longman

Summit: English for Today's World 1

Copyright © 2006 by Pearson Education, Inc.
All rights reserved.
No part of this publication may be reproduced, stored in a retrieval system, or transmitted in any form or by any means, electronic, mechanical, photocopying, recording, or otherwise, without the prior permission of the publisher.

Pearson Education, 10 Bank Street, White Plains, NY 10606

Staff credits: The people who made up the *Summit 1* Student's Book team—representing editorial, production, design, and manufacturing—are Rhea Banker, Peter Benson, Aerin Csigay, Dave Dickey, Pamela Fishman, Ann France, Geraldine Geniusas, Aliza Greenblatt, Ray Keating, Mike Kemper, and Sasha Kintzler.

Text composition: Kirchoff / Wohlberg

Text font: Palatino 11/13

Cover photograph: "Apex," by Rhea Banker. Copyright © 2006 by Rhea Banker.

Illustration credits: Steve Attoe pp. 42, 52, 90, 111; Mark Collins pp. 40, 65, 98; Francois Escalmel pp. 75, 81, 116; Maria LaFrance, p. 10; Marc Mongeau p. 22; Dusan Petricic pp. 30, 101, 105, 118; Craig Spearing p. 68; Eve Steccati p. 104; Jean Wiesenbaugh p. 2

Photo credits: All original photography by David Mager. Page 3 David Zimmerman/Masterfile; p. 8 (top) Denis Scott/Corbis, (left to right) Robert Frerck/Odyssey Productions, Inc., RubberBall/SuperStock, Michael Newman/PhotoEdit, Imageshop-Zefa Visual Media UK Ltd/Alamy, Image100/SuperStock; p. 9 Hulton-Deutsch Collection/Corbis; p. 16 Neal Preston/Corbis; p. 17 Jo Hale/Getty Images; p. 18 (left) Image100/SuperStock, (middle) RubberBall/SuperStock, (right) age fotostock/SuperStock; p. 20 Archivo Iconografico, S.A. /Corbis; p. 21 (left) Lee Celano/Getty Images, (middle) Fox Photos/Getty Images, (right) Bret Thompsett/Alpha/Globe Photos; p. 22 Hemera Technologies/Alamy; p. 26 G. Bliss/Masterfile; p. 27 David Buffington/Getty Images; p. 28 (left to right) Stockbyte, Photomorgana/Corbis, LWA-Dann Tardif/Corbis, BananaStock/Robert Harding; p. 30 Mediacolor's/Alamy; p. 32 Mark E. Gibson/Corbis; p. 33 G. Bliss/Masterfile; p. 34 (left) Camera Press Digital/Retna Ltd., (right) www.newmansown.com; p. 38 (top left) Kaz Mori/Getty Images, (bottom left) Martin Harvey/Alamy, (middle) Reuters/Corbis, (top right) The Art Archive/Musee Carnavalet Paris/Dagli Orti, (top right inset) www.englishcountrydancing.org, (bottom right) Picture Finders Ltd./eStock Photo; p. 39 (left to right) Thinkstock/Alamy, Stadium Studio/Alamy, Royalty-Free/Corbis, Royalty-Free/Corbis; p. 43 (A) Jon Feingersh/Masterfile, (B) Blend Images/Alamy, (C) RubberBall/SuperStock, (D) age fotostock/Medioimages, (E) Pierre Vauthey/Corbis; p. 44 (goatee) Emely/zefa/Corbis, (sideburns) Dennis Galante/Corbis, (buzz) Latin Focus.com, (bald) George Shelley/Corbis, (dyed) Brand X Pictures/Alamy, (long) Mike Powell/Getty Images, (braids) Royalty-Free/Corbis, (highlights) Stockbyte; p. 45 (top left to right) Mauro Fermariello/Photo Researchers, Inc., Apollo/Alamy, Chuck Pefley/Alamy, Getty Images, Cindy Charles/PhotoEdit, (bottom left to right) Gideon Mendel/Corbis, Ariel Skelley/Corbis, Jon Feingersh/Corbis; p. 46 Valentino Maria Chandoha/Corbis Sygma; p. 50 (top) Paul Chesley/National Geographic Image Collection, (bottom) Panoramic Images/Getty Images, (right) Stephanie Maze/Woodfin Camp and Associates; p. 51 (top) Will & Deni McIntyre/Corbis, (bottom) Randy M. Ury/Corbis; p. 52 Christian Zachariasen/Corbis; p. 54 (left to right) Catherine Ledner/Getty Images, Michael Prince/Corbis, age fotostock/Jack Hollingsworth, Roberto Stelzer/Getty Images; p. 56 AP/Wide World Photos; p. 58 (top) Danny Lehman/Corbis, (bottom) age fotostock/SuperStock; p. 62 Private Collection, Archives Charmet/ Bridgeman Art Library; p. 63 Network Photographers/Alamy; p. 66 Ellen Senisi/ The Image Works; p. 67 (parrot) Gerry Ellis/Minden Pictures, (cat) Digital Vision Ltd./SuperStock, (pit bull) Julia Fishkin/Getty Images, (pug) Chris Carlson/Corbis, (python) Michael & Patricia Fogden/Minden Pictures, (mouse) Chris Collins/Corbis; p. 70 (left) Konrad Wothe/Minden Pictures, (right) age fotostock/SuperStock, (bottom) John Cancalosi/naturepl.com; p. 74 (TV) Jimmy Dorantes/Latin Focus.com, (magazine) Image courtesy of The Advertising Archives, (blimp) Shotfile/Alamy, (billboards) Liu Liqun/Corbis, (radio) Joe Tree/Alamy; p. 75 (left) Imagination Photo Design, (middle) Imagination Photo Design, (right) Frank Siteman/Index Stock Imagery; p. 76 Jon Arnold Images/Alamy; p. 77 (perfumes) Raymond Patrick/Getty Images, (chocolates) C Squared Studios/Getty Images, (watches) allOver photography/Alamy, (sunglasses) Darren Robb/Getty Images, (bags) Samsonite Corporation, (umbrellas) Samsonite Corporation; p. 78 (top left) Stockbyte, (top right) Royalty-Free/Corbis, (bottom left) Robert Fried/ robertfriedphotography.com, (bottom right) Robert Fried/ robertfriedphotography.com; 82 Brand X Pictures/Alamy; p. 86 (top) (c)The New Yorker Collection 2004 Lee Lorenz from cartoonbank.com. All rights reserved, (bottom) Marty Bucella http://members.aol.com/mjbtoons/index.html; p. 87 David Young-Wolff/Alamy; p. 88 ER Productions/Corbis; p. 92 (top) Jonathan Smith/Lonely Planet Images, (bottom) Imageshop-Zefa Visual Media UK Ltd/Alamy; p. 94 (top) SCPhotos/Almay, (bottom) View Stock/Alamy; p. 95 (left) Keith Levit Photography/Index Stock Imagery, (middle) age fotostock/Creatas, (right) age fotostock/BananaStock; p. 99 (top) Bettmann/Corbis, (left) Popperfoto/Alamy, (right) WorldAtlas.com/GraphicMaps.com; p. 102 (left) John W. Hoopes, (right) Universtiy of Bologna; p. 103 (left) Richard T. Nowitz/Getty Images, (middle) Yann Arthus-Bertrand/Corbis, (right) David Hardy/Photo Researchers, Inc.; p. 104 Bettmann/Corbis, (inset) Hulton Archive/Getty Images; p. 105 Getty Images; p. 106 (top left) Reuters/Corbis, (top right) AP/Wide World Photos, (left) Popperfoto/Alamy; p. 110 (top left) Image courtesy of The Advertising Archives, (top right) Royalty-Free/Corbis, (middle left) Image courtesy of The Advertising Archives, (middle right) Image courtesy of The Advertising Archives, (bottom left) Peter Cade/Getty Images, (bottom right) Rob Van Petten/Getty Images; p. 112 (go) Royalty-Free/Corbis, (chess) Royalty-Free/Corbis, (video) Michael A. Keller/Corbis, (ping) Agence Images/Alamy, (embroidery) Paul A. Souders/Corbis, (wood) Jim Craigmyle/Masterfile, (crochet) John and Lisa Merrill/Corbis, (karate) Buzz Productions/Alamy, (aerobics) Jose Luis Pelaez, Inc./Corbis, (yoga) Peter Griffith/Masterfile, (antiques) Paul Barton/Corbis, (rabbits) age fotostock/Max Messerli, (coins) Don Farrall/Getty Images; p. 113 (left) John Foxx/Alamy, (middle) Robert Frerck/Odyssey Productions, Inc., (right) Image100/Alamy; p. 115 Dorling Kindersley; p. 118 Chad Slattery/Getty Images; p. 119 (far left) Amy and Chuck Wiley/Wales/Index Stock Imagery, (top left) Rick Doyle/Corbis, (top right) David Madison/Getty Images, (bottom left) Jakob Helbig/Getty Images, (bottom middle) Jess Stock/Getty Images, (bottom right) Joe McBride/Getty Images.

The Library of Congress has cataloged the earlier edition as follows:

Saslow, Joan M.
Summit 1 : English for today's world / Joan Saslow, Allen Ascher.
    p. cm.
1. English language—Textbooks for foreign speakers. 2. English language—Rhetoric. I. Ascher, Allen. II. Title: Summit one. III. Title.
PE1128.S2756 2006
428.2'4--dc22

2005032397

ISBNs 0-13-110625-2 (pbk.)
    0-13-232008-8 (Student's Book with Take-Home Super CD-ROM)

Printed in the United States of America
8 9 10–CRK–11 10 09

Contents

APPENDICES

Scope and Sequence OF CONTENT AND SKILLS

UNIT	Vocabulary*	Conversation Strategies	Discussion Topics	Gramma
1 **New Perspectives** *Page 2*	• Personality types **Word Skill:** classifying by positive and negative meaning	• Ask a question to buy time • Use *Actually* to soften a negative response • Answer a question and then ask a similar one to show interest • Use *I wonder* to elicit an opinion politely • Use *You know* to indicate that you are about to offer advice or a suggestion	• Finding balance in life • Different personality types • Optimism vs. pessimism • Perspectives on life • Life-changing experiences	• Gerunds and infinitives: changes in meaning
2 **Musical Moods** *Page 14*	• Elements of music • Describing creative personalities **Word Skill:** using participial adjectives	• Use *So* to indicate a desire to begin a conversation • Confirm information with *right?* • Use *You know* to introduce information and be less abrupt • Begin answers with *Well* to introduce an opinion	• Musical tastes • The role of music in your life • Creative personalities • The benefits of music • The uses of music therapy	• The present perfect and the present perfect continuous: finished and unfinished actions • Noun clauses
3 **Money Matters** *Page 26*	• Expressing buyer's remorse • Describing spending habits • Charity and investment	• Use *Hey* to indicate enthusiasm • Use *To tell you the truth* to introduce an unexpected assertion • Ask *What do you mean?* to clarify • Provide an example to back up a statement or opinion	• Your financial IQ • Your short-term and long-term financial goals • Buyer's remorse • Spending habits • Charitable giving	• Future plans and finished future actions • The past unreal conditional: inverted form
4 **Looking Good** *Page 38*	• Describing fashion and style **Word Skill:** using the prefix *self-*	• Use *Can you believe* to indicate disapproval • Use *Don't you think* to promote consensus • Begin a response with *Well* to convey polite disagreement or reservation • Stress the main verb to acknowledge only partial agreement	• Appropriate dress • How clothing affects the way others perceive you • Fashions and hairstyles • How men and women change their appearances • The media's influence on body image • Beauty on the outside vs. beauty on the inside	• Quantifiers
5 **Community** *Page 50*	• Ways to soften an objection • Ways to perform community service **Word Skill:** using negative prefixes to form antonyms	• Use *Do you mind* to express concern that an intended action may offend • Use *Actually* to object politely • Use expressions such as *I hope that's not a problem* to soften an objection • Say *Not at all* to indicate a willingness to comply	• Urban life vs. rural life • Behavior in public places • Social responsibility • Urban problems	• Possessives with gerunds • Paired conjunctions

*Vocabulary presentations in *Summit* include individual words, phrases, and collocations.

Grammar and Pronunciation Boosters	Listening Tasks	Readings	Writing
Grammar Booster • Gerunds and infinitives: summary **Grammar for Writing:** parallelism with gerunds and infinitives **Pronunciation Booster** • Content words and function words	• Rephrase descriptions of people • Identify main ideas • Infer what people mean • Categorize people by personality type	• A magazine article about finding balance in life • A magazine article about optimism vs. pessimism	• Describe personality types **Writing Skill:** the paragraph
Grammar Booster • Finished and unfinished actions: summary • The past perfect continuous **Grammar for Writing:** noun clauses as adjective and noun complements **Pronunciation Booster** • Intonation patterns	• Evaluate three pieces of music • Recognize gist before details • Determine benefits and provide examples • Identify points of view	• Brief CD reviews from a website • Interviews: the role of music in one's life • A biography of Ludwig van Beethoven	• Describe yourself **Writing Skill:** parallel structure
Grammar Booster • The future continuous • The future perfect continuous **Pronunciation Booster** • Sentence rhythm: thought groups	• Infer what people mean • Focus on main ideas • Distinguish advice from other information • Summarize problems	• Financial tips from a newspaper • Interviews: financial goals • A magazine article about Paul Newman's philanthropy	• Explain your financial goals **Writing Skill:** sequencing events
Grammar Booster • Quantifiers: *a few* and *few, a little* and *little* • Quantifiers: using *of* • Quantifiers: used without referents **Grammar for Writing:** subject-verb agreement with quantifiers with *of* **Pronunciation Booster** • Linking sounds	• Identify points of view • Rephrase information • Summarize information • Infer what people mean	• A newspaper article about casual dress at work • A magazine article about how the media affects self-image	• Compare two people's tastes in fashion **Writing Skill:** compare and contrast
Grammar Booster • Conjunctions with *so, too, neither,* or *not either*: usage, form, and short responses **Pronunciation Booster** • Unstressed syllables: vowel reduction to /ə/	• Summarize a detailed story • Collaborate to understand details • Infer what people mean	• A graph depicting world population changes • Interviews: pet peeves about public conduct • An interview with Dr. Janice Perlman about "megacities"	• Complain about a problem **Writing Skill:** formal letters

Scope and Sequence OF CONTENT AND SKILLS

UNIT	Vocabulary	Conversation Strategies	Discussion Topics	Grammar
6 **Animals** *Page 62*	• Ways animals are used or treated • Describing pets • Describing character traits	• Use *I've heard* to introduce a statement of popular opinion • Use *For one thing* to provide one reason among several in supporting an argument • Use *Believe it or not* to introduce surprising information	• The treatment of animals • The advantages and disadvantages of different pets • Animal characters in books, cartoons, TV programs, and movies • The value of animal conservation	• The passive voice with modals
7 **Advertising and Consumers** *Page 74*	• Describing low prices and high prices • Shopping expressions • Ways to persuade	• Soften a wish or a statement of intent with *I think* • Ask questions to narrow scope • Say *Of course* to make an affirmative answer stronger	• Appropriate pricing • Smart shopping • Reactions to ads • Advertising techniques • Compulsive shopping	• Passive forms of gerunds and infinitives
8 **Family Trends** *Page 86*	• Examples of bad behavior • Describing parent and teen behavior **Word Skill:** transforming verbs and adjectives into nouns	• Use *I hate to say it, but* to introduce unwelcome information • Respond with *I suppose* to indicate partial agreement • Use *But* to introduce a dissenting opinion	• Conflicts in relationships • Birthrates and life expectancy • Parent–teen issues • Changing family demographics • Generational issues and concerns • Current family trends • Care for the elderly	• Repeated comparatives and double comparatives
9 **History's Mysteries** *Page 98*	• Ways to say "I don't know." • Ways to express certainty **Word Skill:** using adjectives with the suffix *-able*	• Use *Well* to introduce an encouraging statement • Say *You're probably right* to acknowledge another's encouragement • Ask a question with *Why else* to confirm one's own opinion	• Theories that best explain mysteries • The credibility of stories • Trustworthy news sources	• Indirect speech with modals • Perfect modals in the passive voice for speculating about the past
10 **Your Free Time** *Page 110*	• Ways to express fear and fearlessness **Word Skill:** using collocations for leisure activities **Word Skill:** modifying with adverbs	• Use *kind of* to soften an assertion • Use *I hate to say this, but* to excuse oneself for disagreeing • Use *Well, even so* to acknowledge someone's point but disagree politely	• The benefits of leisure activities • Hobbies and interests • Your use of leisure time • Extreme sports • Risk-taking vs. risk-avoidance	• Order of modifiers

Grammar and Pronunciation Boosters	Listening Tasks	Readings	Writing
Grammar Booster • Modals and modal-like expressions: summary **Pronunciation Booster** • Sound reduction	• Rephrase descriptions • Determine the moral of a story • Identify character traits • Focus on details	• The Chinese Zodiac • A discussion board about the humane treatment of animals • An article about animal conservation	• Express an opinion on animal treatment **Writing Skill:** persuasion
Grammar Booster **Grammar for Writing:** past forms of gerunds and infinitives: active and passive voice **Pronunciation Booster** • Vowel sounds /i/ and /ɪ/	• Identify points of view • Rephrase what people are doing • Match advertising techniques to ads • Determine people's attitudes	• Interviews: reactions to ads • A presentation of eight advertising techniques • A magazine article about compulsive shopping	• Explain an article you read **Writing Skill:** writing a summary
Grammar Booster • Making comparisons: summary • Other uses of comparatives, superlatives, and comparisons with *as . . . as* **Pronunciation Booster** • Stress placement: prefixes and suffixes	• Summarize demographic information • Rephrase people's points of view • Focus on details • Classify information to compare two generations • Apply logic to information	• A brochure about falling birthrates • A newspaper article about China's elderly population • Case studies: aging parents	• Describe your relationship with a family member **Writing Skill:** avoiding comma splices and run-on sentences
Grammar Booster • Reporting verbs *say*, *ask*, and *tell*: summary **Grammar for Writing:** other reporting verbs **Pronunciation Booster** • Reduction and linking in perfect modals in the passive voice	• Summarize main ideas • Identify information that supports an argument • Infer what people mean	• "The World's Easiest Quiz" • Descriptions of Bigfoot, the Loch Ness Monster, and the Bermuda Triangle • Encyclopedia entries about well-known mysteries • A magazine article about the world's greatest hoaxes	• Write a news article **Writing Skill:** avoiding sentence fragments
Grammar Booster • Intensifiers • Adverbs of manner **Pronunciation Booster** • Vowel sounds /eɪ/, /ɛ/, /æ/, and /ʌ/	• Classify information to define terms • Match activities with people, according to the information they imply	• Statistics comparing technological promises vs. reality • Case studies: stressful situations • Message-board posts about unusual hobbies • A magazine article about technology and leisure time	• Comment on another's point of view **Writing Skill:** expressing and supporting your opinion

International Advisory Board

The authors gratefully acknowledge the substantive and formative contributions of the members of the International Advisory Board.

CHERYL BELL
Middlesex County College, Middlesex, New Jersey, USA

ELMA CABAHUG
City College of San Francisco, San Francisco, California, USA

JO CARAGATA
Mukogawa Women's University, Hyogo, Japan

ANN CARTIER
Palo Alto Adult School, Palo Alto, California, USA

TERRENCE FELLNER
Himeji Dokkyo University, Hyogo, Japan

JOHN FUJIMORI
Meiji Gakuin High School, Tokyo, Japan

ARETA ULHANA GALAT
Escola Superior de Estudos Empresariais e Informática,
Curitiba, Brazil

DOREEN M. GAYLORD
Kanazawa Technical College, Ishikawa, Japan

EMILY GEHRMAN
Newton International College, Garden Grove, California, USA

ANN-MARIE HADZIMA
National Taiwan University, Taipei, Taiwan

KAREN KYONG-AI PARK
Seoul National University, Seoul, Korea

ANA PATRICIA MARTÍNEZ VITE DIP. R.S.A.
Universidad del Valle de México, Mexico City, Mexico

MICHELLE ANN MERRITT
Proulex/Universidad de Guadalajara, Guadalajara, Mexico

ADRIANNE P. OCHOA
Georgia State University, Atlanta, Georgia, USA

LOUIS PARDILLO
Korea Herald English Institute, Seoul, Korea

THELMA PERES
Casa Thomas Jefferson, Brasília, Brazil

DIANNE RUGGIERO
Broward Community College, Davie, Florida, USA

KEN SCHMIDT
Tohoku Fukushi University, Sendai, Japan

ALISA A. TAKEUCHI
Garden Grove Adult Education, Garden Grove, California, USA

JOSEPHINE TAYLOR
Centro Colombo Americano, Bogotá, Colombia

PATRICIA VECIÑO
Instituto Cultural Argentino Norteamericano,
Buenos Aires, Argentina

FRANCES WESTBROOK
AUA Language Center, Bangkok, Thailand

Reviewers and Piloters Many thanks also to the reviewers and piloters all over the world who reviewed *Top Notch* and *Summit* in their final forms.

G. Julian Abaqueta, Huachiew Chalermprakiet University, Samutprakarn, Thailand • **David Aline**, Kanagawa University, Kanagawa, Japan • **Marcia Alves**, Centro Cultural Brasil Estados Unidos, Franca, Brazil • **Yousef Al-Yacoub**, Qatar Petroleum, Doha, Qatar • **Maristela Barbosa Silveira e Silva**, Instituto Cultural Brasil-Estados Unidos, Manaus, Brazil • **Beth Bartlett**, Centro Colombo Americano, Cali, Colombia • **Carla Battigelli**, University of Zulia, Maracaibo, Venezuela • **Claudia Bautista**, C.B.C., Caracas, Venezuela • **Rob Bell**, Shumei Yachiyo High School, Chiba, Japan • **Dr. Maher Ben Moussa**, Sharjah University, Sharjah, United Arab Emirates • **Elaine Cantor**, Englewood Senior High School, Jacksonville, Florida, USA • **María Aparecida Capellari**, SENAC, São Paulo, Brazil • **Eunice Carrillo Ramos**, Colegio Durango, Naucalpan, Mexico • **Janette Carvalhinho de Oliveira**, Centro de Linguas (UFES), Vitória, Brazil • **María Amelia Carvalho Fonseca**, Centro Cultural Brasil-Estados Unidos, Belém, Brazil • **Audy Castañeda**, Instituto Pedagógico de Caracas, Caracas, Venezuela • **Ching-Fen Chang**, National Chiao Tung University, Hsinchu, Taiwan • **Ying-Yu Chen**, Chinese Culture University, Taipei, Taiwan • **Joyce Chin**, The Language Training and Testing Center, Taipei, Taiwan • **Eun Cho**, Pagoda Language School, Seoul, Korea • **Hyungzung Cho**, MBC Language Institute, Seoul, Korea • **Dong Sua Choi**, MBC Language Institute, Seoul, Korea • **Jeong Mi Choi**, Freelancer, Seoul, Korea • **Peter Chun**, Pagoda Language School, Seoul, Korea • **Eduardo Corbo**, Legacy ELT, Salto, Uruguay • **Marie Cosgrove**, Surugadai University, Saitama, Japan • **María Antonieta Covarrubias Souza**, Centro Escolar Akela, Mexico City, Mexico • **Katy Cox**, Casa Thomas Jefferson, Brasília, Brazil • **Michael Donovan**, Gakushuin University, Tokyo, Japan • **Stewart Dorward**, Shumei Eiko High School, Saitama, Japan • **Ney Eric Espina**, Centro Venezolano Americano del Zulia, Maracaibo, Venezuela • **Edith Espino**, Centro Especializado de Lenguas - Universidad Tecnológica de Panamá, El Dorado, Panama • **Allen P. Fermon**, Instituto Brasil-Estados Unidos, Ceará, Brazil • **Simão Ferreira Banha**, Phil Young's English School, Curitiba, Brazil • **María Elena Flores Lara**, Colegio Mercedes, Mexico City, Mexico • **Valesca Fróis Nassif**, Associação Cultural Brasil-Estados Unidos, Salvador, Brazil • **José Fuentes**, Empire Language Consulting, Caracas, Venezuela • **José Luis Guerrero**, Colegio Cristóbal Colón, Mexico City, Mexico • **Claudia Patricia Gutiérrez**, Centro Colombo Americano, Cali, Colombia • **Valerie Hansford**, Asia University, Tokyo, Japan • **Gene Hardstark**, Dotkyo University, Saitama, Japan • **Maiko Hata**, Kansai University, Osaka, Japan • **Susan Elizabeth Haydock Miranda de Araujo**, Centro Cultural Brasil Estados Unidos, Belém, Brazil • **Gabriela Herrera**, Fundametal, Valencia, Venezuela • **Sandy Ho**, GEOS International, New York, New York, USA • **Yuri Hosoda**, Showa Women's University, Tokyo, Japan • **Hsiao-I Hou**, Shu-Te University, Kaohsiung County, Taiwan • **Kuei-ping Hsu**, National Tsing Hua University, Hsinchu, Taiwan • **Chia-yu Huang**, National Tsing Hua University, Hsinchu, Taiwan • **Caroline C. Hwang**, National Taipei University of Science and Technology, Taipei, Taiwan • **Diana Jones**, Angloamericano, Mexico City, Mexico • **Eunjeong Kim**, Freelancer, Seoul, Korea • **Julian Charles King**, Qatar Petroleum, Doha, Qatar • **Bruce Lee**, CIE: Foreign Language Institute, Seoul, Korea • **Myunghee Lee**, MBC Language Institute, Seoul, Korea • **Naidnapa Leoprasertkul**, Language Development Center, Mahasarakham University, Mahasarakham, Thailand • **Eleanor S. Leu**, Souchow University, Taipei, Taiwan • **Eliza Liu**, Chinese Culture University, Taipei, Taiwan • **Carlos Lizárraga**, Angloamericano, Mexico City, Mexico • **Philippe Loussarevian**, Keio University Shonan Fujisawa High School, Kanagawa, Japan • **Jonathan Lynch**, Azabu University, Tokyo, Japan • **Thomas Mach**, Konan University, Hyogo, Japan • **Lilian Mandel Civatti**, Associação Cultural Brasil-Estados Unidos, Salvador, Brazil • **Hakan Mansuroglu**, Zoni Language Center, West New York, New Jersey, USA • **Martha McGaughey**, Language Training Institute, Englewood Cliffs, New Jersey, USA • **David Mendoza Plascencia**, Instituto Internacional de Idiomas, Naucalpan, Mexico • **Theresa Mezo**, Interamerican University, Río Piedras, Puerto Rico • **Luz Adriana Montenegro Silva**, Colegio CAFAM, Bogotá, Colombia • **Magali de Moraes Menti**, Instituto Lingua, Porto Alegre, Brazil • **Massoud Moslehpour**, The Overseas Chinese Institute of Technology, Taichung, Taiwan • **Jennifer Nam**, IKE, Seoul, Korea • **Marcos Norelle F. Victor**, Instituto Brasil-Estados Unidos, Ceará, Brazil • **Luz María Olvera**, Instituto Juventud del Estado de México, Naucalpan, Mexico • **Roxana Orrego Ramírez**, Universidad Diego Portales, Santiago, Chile • **Ming-Jong Pan**, National Central University, Jhongli City, Taiwan • **Sandy Park**, Topia Language School, Seoul, Korea • **Patrícia Elizabeth Peres Martins**, Instituto Brasil-Estados Unidos, Rio de Janeiro, Brazil • **Rodrigo Peza**, Passport Language Centers, Bogotá, Colombia • **William Porter**, Osaka Institute of Technology, Osaka, Japan • **Caleb Prichard**, Kwansei Gakuin University, Hyogo, Japan • **Mirna Quintero**, Instituto Pedagógico de Caracas, Caracas, Venezuela • **Roberto Rabbini**, Seigakuin University, Saitama, Japan • **Terri Rapoport**, Berkeley College, White Plains, New York, USA • **Yvette Rieser**, Centro Electrónico de Idiomas, Maracaibo, Venezuela • **Orlando Rodríguez**, New English Teaching School, Paysandu, Uruguay • **Mayra Rosario**, Pontificia Universidad Católica Madre y Maestra, Santiago, Dominican Republic • **Peter Scout**, Sakura no Seibo Junior College, Fukushima, Japan • **Jungyeon Shim**, EG School, Seoul, Korea • **Keum Ok Song**, MBC Language Institute, Seoul, Korea • **Assistant Professor Dr. Reongrudee Soonthornmanee**, Chulalongkorn University Language Institute, Bangkok, Thailand • **Claudia Stanisclause**, The Language College, Maracay, Venezuela • **Tom Suh**, The Princeton Review, Seoul, Korea • **Phiphawin Suphawat**, KhonKaen University, KhonKaen, Thailand • **Craig Sweet**, Poole Gakuin Junior and Senior High Schools, Osaka, Japan • **Yi-nien Josephine Twu**, National Tsing Hua University, Hsinchu, Taiwan • **Maria Christina Uchôa Close**, Instituto Cultural Brasil-Estados Unidos, São José dos Campos, Brazil • **Luz Vanegas Lopera**, Lexicom The Place For Learning English, Medellín, Colombia • **Julieta Vasconcelos García**, Centro Escolar del Lago, A.C., Mexico City, Mexico • **Carol Vaughan**, Kanto Kokusai High School, Tokyo, Japan • **Patricia Celia Veciño**, Instituto Cultural Argentino Norteamericano, Buenos Aires, Argentina • **Isabela Villas Boas**, Casa Thomas Jefferson, Brasília, Brazil • **Iole Vitti**, Peanuts English School, Poços de Caldas, Brazil • **Gabi Witthaus**, Qatar Petroleum, Doha, Qatar • **Yi-Ling Wu**, Shih Chien University, Taipei, Taiwan • **Chad Wynne**, Osaka Keizai University, Osaka, Japan • **Belkis Yanes**, Freelance Instructor, Caracas, Venezuela • **I-Chieh Yang**, Chung-kuo Institute of Technology, Taipei, Taiwan • **Emil Ysona**, Instituto Cultural Dominico-Americano, Santo Domingo, Dominican Republic • **Chi-fang Yu**, Soo Chow University, Taipei, Taiwan, • **Shigeki Yusa**, Sendai Shirayuri Women's College, Sendai, Japan

—— *In memory of Rob Bell* ——

To the Teacher

What is *Summit*?

- *Summit* is a two-level high-intermediate to advanced communicative series for adults and young adults that can follow any intermediate course book.
- *Summit* is designed to follow the *Top Notch* series, forming the top two levels of a six-level course.
- Each *Summit* Student's Book is designed for 60 to 90 instructional hours with options and extensions that enable it to fulfill the needs of longer courses.

Key Elements of the *Summit* Instructional Design

Concise two-page lessons

Each easy-to-teach two-page lesson is designed for one class session and begins with a clearly stated communication goal and ends with free communication practice. Each lesson integrates all four skills with a focus on conversation, grammar, reading, or listening, keeping the pace of a class session lively and varied.

Daily confirmation of progress

Adult students need to observe and confirm their own progress. In *Summit*, students conclude each class session with a culminating productive activity that demonstrates their ability to use new vocabulary, grammar, word skills, and social language in order to perform the communication goal of the lesson. This motivates students and keeps them eager to continue their study of English, and it builds their pride in being able to speak and write accurately, fluently, and authentically.

Real language

Carefully exposing students to authentic, natural, corpus-informed English, both receptively and productively, is a necessary component of building understanding and expression. All Conversation Snapshots and Sound Bites feature the language people *really* use; nowhere to be found is "textbook English" written merely to exemplify grammar.

Memorable model conversations

Even at the advanced levels, learners need models of social language plus strategies they can use conversationally. The full range of social and functional communicative needs as well as a wealth of conversation strategies are presented through practical model conversations that are intensively practiced and applied to the learner's own life experience. Rhythm and intonation practice and an optional Pronunciation Booster provide targeted practice to ensure clear expression.

High-impact vocabulary syllabus

In order to ensure students' solid acquisition of vocabulary essential for communication, *Summit* contains explicit presentation and practice of words, collocations, and expressions appropriate at each level of study. A focus on word skills, such as using prefixes and participial adjectives, builds students' ability to cope with and expand on new vocabulary. Meaning is conveyed in a variety of ways: through captioned photographs and illustrations, within the context of realia and readings, in definitions and contextualized sentences, and in authentic dictionary entries from the *Longman Advanced American Dictionary*. These presentations provide a permanent in-book reference that builds learner independence and helps students prepare for tests.

Learner-supportive grammar

Grammar is approached explicitly and cognitively, through form, meaning, and use, in the following places in *Summit*: in every Student's Book unit, in the bound-in Grammar Booster, in the *Summit* Workbook, in the optional worksheets provided on the Teacher's Resource Disk (found in the Teacher's Edition and Lesson Planner), and on the *Summit* companion website. Grammar charts provide examples and paradigms enhanced by simple usage notes at students' level of comprehension. This takes the guesswork out of meaning, makes lesson preparation easier for teachers, and provides students with comprehensible charts for permanent reference and test preparation. All presentations of grammar, both in the Student's Book and in the Grammar Booster, include exercises to ensure adequate practice.

Detailed writing syllabus

The *Summit* Student's Book contains a writing syllabus that includes rigorous practice and clear models of important rhetorical and mechanical writing skills, such as parallelism, summarizing, and punctuation. Each lesson provides practice in the writing process, from prewriting to revision.

Unique discussion syllabus

All students want and need to participate in real discussions. *Summit* systematically goes beyond conversation model practice through unique step-by-step Discussion Builders that enable students to prepare for successful discourse. This preparation results in increased accuracy, increased fluency, greater complexity of expression, richer use of vocabulary, and much less fossilization. The Teacher's Resource Disk offers further optional practice with Discourse Strategies to ensure successful communication.

Components of *Summit 1*

Student's Book with Take-Home Super CD-ROM

The Student's Book contains a bound-in Grammar Booster, a bound-in Pronunciation Booster, and a Take-Home Super CD-ROM. The Super CD-ROM provides a variety of exciting interactive activities, including speaking practice, listening comprehension, reading comprehension, an interactive workbook, and games and puzzles. The disk can also be played on an audio CD player to listen to the conversation models and for intensive pronunciation practice.

Teacher's Edition and Lesson Planner

The Teacher's Edition and Lesson Planner offers complete lesson plans for each class session. Suggested teaching times are included for each activity to take the guesswork out of planning. Bound into each Teacher's Edition and Lesson Planner is a free Teacher's Resource Disk with the following optional printable activities to personalize your teaching style:

- Vocabulary-Building Strategies
- Discourse Strategies
- Listening Strategies
- Reading Strategies
- Grammar Self-Checks
- Conversation Prompts
- Extra Writing Skills Practice
- Pronunciation Activities

- A Reading Speed Calculator
- Extra Reading Comprehension Activities
- Graphic Organizers

Complete Class Audio Program

The Class Audio Program contains listening comprehension activities, rhythm and intonation practice, and targeted pronunciation activities that focus on accurate and comprehensible pronunciation.

Because *Summit* is a course for international communication, a variety of native *and* non-native speakers are included to prepare students for the world outside the classroom.

Workbook

The tightly linked, illustrated Workbook contains exercises that provide additional practice and reinforcement of language concepts and skills from *Summit* and its Grammar Booster.

Complete Assessment Package with Exam*View*® Software

Ten easy-to-administer and simple-to-score unit achievement tests assess listening, vocabulary, grammar, social language, reading, and writing. Two review tests, one mid-book and one end-of-book, provide additional cumulative assessment. A speaking test and a writing test are included with each review. In addition to the photocopiable achievement tests, Exam*View*® software enables teachers to tailor-make tests to best meet their needs by combining items any way they wish.

Summit TV

An engrossing and informative video offers excerpts from authentic TV documentaries as well as unrehearsed on-the-street interviews with English speakers from around the world. Both the documentaries and the interviews are thematically tied to the *Summit* units in order to initiate and promote classroom discussion.

Summit Companion Website

The *Summit* Companion Website www.longman.com/summit provides numerous additional resources for students and teachers. This no-cost, high-benefit feature includes opportunities for further practice of language and content from the *Summit* Student's Book.

Welcome to Summit!

About the Authors

JOAN SASLOW is author of a number of textbook series for adults and young adults, including *Ready to Go: Language, Lifeskills, and Civics*, a four-level adult ESL series; *Workplace Plus: Living and Working in English*, a vocational English series; *Literacy Plus*, a two-level series that teaches literacy, English, and culture to adult pre-literate students; and *English in Context: Reading Comprehension for Science and Technology*, a three-level series for English for special purposes.

Ms. Saslow is co-author, with Allen Ascher, of *Top Notch: English for Today's World*. She was the Series Director of *True Colors: An EFL Course for Real Communication* and of *True Voices*, a five-level EFL video course. Ms. Saslow's special interest is in distinguishing the needs of the EFL and the ESL learner and creating materials appropriate for each.

Ms. Saslow has taught in Chile and the United States in a variety of programs. In Chile, she taught English and French at the Binational Centers of Valparaíso and Viña del Mar, and at the Catholic University of Valparaíso. In the United States, Ms. Saslow taught English as a Foreign Language to Japanese university students at Marymount College's intensive English program as well as workplace English at the General Motors auto assembly plant, both in Tarrytown, New York. Ms. Saslow is also an editor, a teacher-trainer, a language learner, and a frequent speaker at gatherings of English teachers throughout the world. Ms. Saslow has an M.A. in French from the University of Wisconsin.

ALLEN ASCHER, formerly Academic Director of the International English Language Institute at Hunter College in New York, has been a teacher, a teacher-trainer, an author, and a publisher. He has taught in language and teacher-training programs in both China and the United States. Mr. Ascher specialized in teaching listening and speaking to students at the Beijing Second Foreign Language Institute, to hotel workers at a major international hotel in China, and to Japanese students from Chubu University studying English at Ohio University in the United States. In New York, Mr. Ascher taught students of all language backgrounds and abilities at the City University of New York, and he trained teachers in the TESOL Certificate Program at the New School. Mr. Ascher has an M.A. in Applied Linguistics from Ohio University.

Mr. Ascher is co-author, with Joan Saslow, of *Top Notch: English for Today's World*. He is author of *Think About Editing: A Grammar Editing Guide for ESL Writers*. As a publisher, Mr. Ascher played a key role in the creation of some of the most widely used materials for adults, including *True Colors, NorthStar, Focus on Grammar, Global Links*, and *Ready to Go*. Mr. Ascher has provided lively workshops for teachers throughout the United States, Asia, Latin America, Europe, and the Middle East.

UNIT 1

New Perspectives

UNIT GOALS

1 Suggest ways to enjoy life more
2 Describe people's personalities
3 Compare perspectives on life
4 Share a life-changing experience

A **Topic Preview.** Look at the map of the world. Where do you think the artist is from?

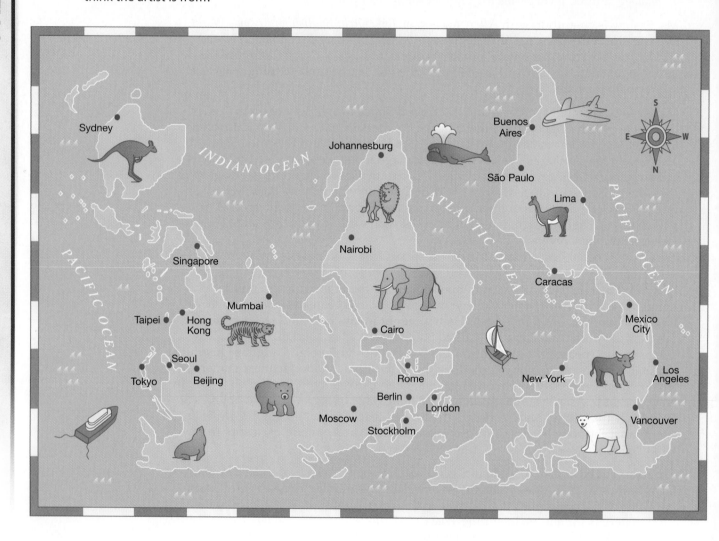

B **Discussion.**

1. What is unusual about the way the map depicts the world?

2. What do you think the artist is trying to say with the illustration? Is the artist being serious or funny?

C 🎧 **Sound Bites.** Read and listen to a conversation between two colleagues working temporarily in another country.

GILBERT: Oh, man! Am I ready to head home!
ANNA: Are you kidding? I can't get enough of this place.
GILBERT: Well, it's been three weeks, and I think I've had about enough. I'm tired of eating strange food.
ANNA: Wow! I feel just the opposite. I can't get over how much I enjoy being here. I love how different the food is.
GILBERT: Well, not me. And frankly, it's a pain in the neck having to work so hard to understand what people are saying to me.
ANNA: I actually think it's fun trying to figure out how to communicate. Stop complaining! You'll be home before you know it!
GILBERT: Fine by me. There's no place like home.

D **In Other Words.** Read the conversation again. With a partner, explain the meaning of each of the following statements.

1. "Am I ready to head home!"
2. "I can't get enough of this place."
3. "I think I've had about enough."
4. "I can't get over how much I enjoy being here."
5. "It's a pain in the neck having to work so hard."
6. "There's no place like home."

E **Pair Work.** Read each statement and decide who you think said it—Anna or Gilbert. Support your opinion with information from the conversation.

"I'm a little uncomfortable with places that are new to me."

"I love trying new things."

"I prefer to stick closer to home."

"I want some adventure in my life."

F **Discussion.**

1. How would you describe Anna's and Gilbert's personalities? How are they different?
2. Who are *you* more like, Gilbert or Anna?

STARTING **POINT**

Pair Work. How do you each feel about travel? Complete the statement to reflect your own opinions. Explain why.

In my opinion, travel can be . . .

☐ a life-changing experience.	☐ pretty dull.	☐ more trouble than it's worth.
☐ kind of scary.	☐ an adventure.	☐ other: ....

1 Suggest ways to enjoy life more

A ∩ GRAMMAR **SNAPSHOT.** Read the article and notice the use of <u>forget</u>, <u>stop</u>, and <u>remember</u>.

Finding Balance

Are you burning the candle at both ends? Do you feel you have no time for yourself? Do you **forget to call** family on birthdays or holidays? Have you **stopped going out** with friends because you're too busy? Do you have trouble relaxing and having fun?

If you recognize yourself, you should **remember to slow down** and **take** more time for everything. Living a balanced life is about integrating the many vital areas of your life, including your health, friends, family, work, and romance.

Here are some tips for restoring a healthy perspective. First, **remember to make** time for the important people in your life. **Stop over-scheduling** and spend quality time with friends and family. Second, learn to eat, talk, walk, and drive more slowly. And **don't forget to turn** your cell phone **off** sometimes. People who really want to talk to you will call back. Third, learn to live in the present and **stop worrying** about the future. And finally, take it easy and begin enjoying the simple things in life. **Stop to smell** the roses.

B Discussion.

1. Did you recognize yourself or someone you know in the article? Give examples.
2. Did you find the tips helpful? Why or why not?

C **Grammar.** **Gerunds and infinitives: changes in meaning**

Some verbs are followed by either a gerund or an infinitive with no change in meaning,
for example: <u>love</u>, <u>hate</u>, <u>can't stand</u>, <u>like</u>, <u>prefer</u>, <u>begin</u>, <u>start</u>, <u>continue</u>.

> **Begin enjoying** the simple things in life. OR **Begin to enjoy** the simple things in life.

Some verbs change meaning, depending on whether they are followed by a gerund or an infinitive.

> <u>remember</u> + infinitive = remember to do something
> **Remember to make** time for the important people in your life.
> I have to **remember to send** an e-mail to my friend.

> <u>remember</u> + gerund = remember something that happened in the past
> I **remember having** more time for myself.
> Do you **remember going** there when you were a kid?

> <u>forget</u> + infinitive = forget to do something
> **Don't forget to turn** your cell phone off.
> He always **forgets to call** on my birthday.

> <u>forget</u> + gerund = forget something that happened in the past
> I'll never **forget seeing** the mountains for the first time.
> Can you ever **forget going** to the beach?

> <u>stop</u> + infinitive = stop in order to do something
> **Stop to smell** the roses.
> Can you **stop to pick up** some chocolates for the party?

> <u>stop</u> + gerund = stop an ongoing action
> **Stop over-scheduling** and spend quality time with friends and family.
> You need to **stop worrying** so much.

> **REMEMBER**
>
> **Some verbs are followed by infinitives.**
> Learn to live in the present.
>
> **Some verbs are followed by gerunds.**
> I enjoy spending time with my friends.
>
> **Some verbs are followed by objects and infinitives.**
> He reminded me to call my mother.
>
> **For a complete list of verbs followed by gerunds, infinitives, and objects and infinitives, see page A3 in the Appendices.**

PAGE G1
For more …

D Complete each sentence with a gerund or an infinitive.

1. I'll never forget (travel) .... abroad for the first time.

2. When I feel stressed out, I remember (put) .... things in perspective.

3. You need to stop (try) .... to do everything at once.

4. If I forget (send) .... a card for a friend's birthday, I try to remember (call) ....

5. We forgot (buy) .... flowers, so we stopped (pick up) .... some on the way to the party.

6. I remember (celebrate) .... holidays with my family when I was young.

GRAMMAR **EXCHANGE** • *Now suggest ways to enjoy life more.*

Pair Work. Write a list of suggestions on your
notepad for what someone can do to enjoy life
more. Use <u>remember</u>, <u>forget</u>, and <u>stop</u>.

Stop worrying about the small things.

Group Work. Share your ideas with your
class. Create a list of suggestions that everyone
agrees with.

2 Describe people's personalities

A ⌒ CONVERSATION **SNAPSHOT**

A: Have you had a chance to meet the new manager?

B: Liz? Actually, no. Have you?

A: Not yet. I wonder what she's like.

B: Well, everyone says she's bad news.

A: You know, you can't believe everything you hear. She might turn out to be a real sweetheart.

⌒ **Rhythm and intonation practice**

B ⌒ Vocabulary. Personality types. Listen and practice.

Positive	Negative
a sweetheart someone who is likable and easy to get along with	**a tyrant** someone, especially a boss, who makes people work extremely hard
a team player someone who works well with other people so the whole group is successful	**a workaholic** someone who is always working and does not have time for anything else
a brain someone who is intelligent and can solve problems that are difficult for others	**a pain in the neck** someone who complains a lot and often causes problems
a people person someone who likes being with and works well with other people	**a wise guy** someone who says or does annoying things, especially to make himself or herself seem smarter than other people

PAGE P1
Content words and
function words

C ⌒ Listening Comprehension. Listen carefully to the conversations about people's personalities. Infer which expression the speaker would use to describe the person.

1. The woman thinks that Shelly is ....
   a. a sweetheart **b.** a brain **c.** a pain in the neck

2. The woman thinks that Peter is ....
   a. a workaholic **b.** a tyrant **c.** a team player

3. The man thinks that Paul is ....
   a. a team player **b.** a people person **c.** a wise guy

D **Word Skills.** **Classifying by positive and negative meaning.** Fill in the diagram with the adjectives in the box. Decide which adjectives describe personalities positively, negatively, or both. Add other adjectives you know.

annoying	funny	lovable	outgoing	silly
easygoing	hardworking	modest	professional	smart
friendly	helpful	nervous	reliable	talkative
fun	impolite	offensive	serious	unfair

Positive   **Both**   **Negative**

E **Pair Work.** With a partner, write adjectives from the chart you think match each of the personality types. More than one answer is possible. Explain your choices.

1. a sweetheart ....
2. a team player ....
3. a brain ....
4. a pain in the neck ....
5. a tyrant ....
6. a wise guy ....
7. a people person ....
8. a workaholic ....

CONVERSATION **STARTER** • *Now describe people's personalities.*

Pair Work. Describe the personalities of people you know, using the vocabulary from page 6 and other adjectives. Give specific examples to explain.

IDEAS

a boss	a friend
a co-worker	a neighbor
a spouse	a teacher
a classmate	a relative

"My sister is such a tyrant! She makes her kids do all the housework!"

"My friend Hugo is a real people person. He's so outgoing and friendly."

Role Play. Role-play a conversation about a person you haven't met yet. Use the Conversation Snapshot on page 6 as a guide. Start like this: "Have you had a chance to meet . . . ?"

3 *Compare perspectives on life*

A **Reading Warm-up.** Look at the glass of water. Do you see the glass as half full or half empty? What does that say about your perspective on life?

B 🎧 **Reading.** Read the article about optimism. How do optimists and pessimists respond to problems differently?

Maintaining a Positive Perspective

by Kali Munro, M.Ed., Psychotherapist

Have you ever wondered why some people feel down and defeated when faced with difficult situations, while others feel challenged and hopeful? These different reactions are due to how people interpret events—whether they think positively, from an optimistic viewpoint, or negatively, from a pessimistic viewpoint.

Optimists and Pessimists

The difference between optimists and pessimists isn't a difference in life experiences but rather in how people perceive and respond to problems. For example, an optimist who is going through a hard time feels confident that life will get better, while a pessimist is more cynical and believes life will always be difficult and painful. Pessimists tend to expect the worst and see only problems. Optimists, confronted with the same situations, expect the best. While a pessimist may give up, an optimist will look on the bright side and, instead of seeing a problem, will see a solution.

The Pros and Cons

There are pros and cons to both optimism and pessimism. A healthy dose of optimism can be uplifting and hopeful, while a healthy dose of pessimism can be realistic and wise. Achieving a balance of being realistic and hopeful isn't always easy.

Staying Optimistic

While we can learn from both optimists and pessimists, most of us need help being optimistic. Maintaining a hopeful, positive, yet realistic perspective in the face of hard times can be a real challenge—one many are facing right now in the world—but it is essential to living peacefully and happily. Just as it is important to recognize what is unjust and unfair in our lives and the world, it is important to see the beauty, love, generosity, and goodness as well.

Source: www.KaliMunro.com

C **Discussion.**

1. Do you agree with the author that "most of us need help being optimistic"? How do you think people can avoid negative thinking? Describe experiences from your own life.

2. In your opinion, are there times when optimism can be bad, or when pessimism can be good? Explain.

D **Pair Work.** How optimistic or pessimistic do you think these people are? Rate them on a scale of 1 to 5 (1 being very optimistic and 5 being very pessimistic). Circle the number. Explain your answers.

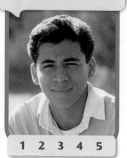

I wouldn't say that I'm cynical, but it's important to be realistic. Let's face it—life is hard.

1 2 3 4 5

I think I can keep things in perspective. I try not to think negatively, but I'm realistic about the things I can't change.

1 2 3 4 5

I try to look on the bright side. I think it's better to try to see a solution instead of seeing a problem.

1 2 3 4 5

I find it difficult when things get tough. I sometimes feel completely hopeless. I just don't expect things to get better.

1 2 3 4 5

I've had some bad experiences, but I think they've made me more realistic. It's not always possible to hope for the best, but good things *do* happen.

1 2 3 4 5

Step 1. Complete the survey.

Do you have a negative or positive perspective?

1. You wake up in the middle of the night with a stomachache. Your first thought is . . .

1pt "I'm sure it's nothing."

2pts "I'll take some medicine."

3pts "I think I should go to the doctor."

2. You apply for your "perfect" job, but you don't get it. You think . . .

1pt "Never mind. I'll find something else."

2pts "That's really unfair."

3pts "It figures. I never get the job I want."

3. When you are introduced to someone new, you . . .

1pt make friends easily with that person.

2pts "warm up" to that person gradually.

3pts make that person prove to you that he or she is likable.

4. News about crime or disasters makes you . . .

1pt want to do something to help.

2pts realize that sometimes bad things happen.

3pts feel unsafe and depressed.

5. When a friend feels down, you . . .

1pt understand and try to offer support.

2pts tell him or her about your problems too.

3pts tell him or her how much worse it could be.

6. Your boss asks you out to lunch. You think . . .

1pt "I must be getting a raise."

2pts "That's really nice."

3pts "Oh, no! I'm getting fired!"

7. If someone unexpectedly knocks on your door, you think . . .

1pt "I wonder which friend is dropping by."

2pts "I wonder who it could be."

3pts "I'm not answering. It must be a salesperson."

Add up your points.

7–10   You're an optimist. You always see the glass half full.

11–14   You're a bit of an optimist and a pessimist. You're very realistic.

15–21   You're a pessimist. You tend to see the glass half empty.

Step 2. Pair Work. Compare and explain your responses to the survey items. Does your score describe you and your perspective on life? Why or why not?

Step 3. Discussion.

1. In your opinion, in order to succeed, how important is your perspective on life? Do you think it's better to be optimistic, pessimistic, or somewhere in the middle? Explain.

2. Read the quotation by Winston Churchill. Do you agree with him? Why or why not?

"The pessimist sees difficulty in every opportunity. The optimist sees the opportunity in every difficulty."

Winston Churchill,
British Prime Minister
(1874–1965)

4 Share a life-changing experience

A 🎧 **Listening Comprehension.** Listen to each person talking about a life-changing experience. Then choose the best answer to complete each statement.

1. The most significant experience of the first speaker's life was when he ....
   a. became a father
   b. began working
   c. traveled to another country
   d. got married

2. The second speaker's life changed when she ....
   a. got a full-time job
   b. had a baby
   c. got more free time
   d. got married

3. The third speaker's perspective on life changed when he ....
   a. lost his home in a fire
   b. lost his job
   c. got divorced
   d. had a serious illness

B 🎧 **Understanding Meaning from Context.** Read the statements. Then listen again to infer what each speaker means.

1. When the first speaker says, "I was really able to see other people's points of view," he means that ....
   a. he could understand how other people feel about things
   b. he met people of different nationalities

2. When the first speaker says, "It was a real eye-opener for me," he means that ....
   a. the experience was a bit scary
   b. the experience taught him a lot

3. When the second speaker says, "It hit me that I was responsible for her," she means that ....
   a. she realized she had to take care of her baby
   b. she regretted she had to take care of her baby

4. When the second speaker says, "[It] is definitely a life-altering experience," she means that ....
   a. the experience is not rewarding
   b. the experience changes a person

5. When the third speaker says, "That put things in perspective," he means that ....
   a. he realized some things are not so important
   b. he had to work day in and day out

6. When the third speaker says, "You start to see the big picture," he means that ....
   a. he understood what was really important in life
   b. he realized how much he had lost

C **Discussion.** In your own words, summarize each person's life-changing experience from the listening. Which person's experience can you identify with the most? Why?

Step 1. Pair Work. What are some experiences that can change a person's perspective on life? Complete the list with your partner.

Things that can change one's perspective
-the birth of a child
-a disaster
-travel

Step 2. Think about a life-changing experience *you* have had. Take notes about it on your notepad.

What was the experience? When did it happen? Where?

How did the experience change your perspective? How did you feel at the time?

Step 3. Group Work. Share your life-changing experience with your classmates. Explain how this experience changed your perspective on life.

"Last year my mother had a serious illness. It really put things in perspective for me. All the disagreements we'd had in the past seemed so unimportant."

"A few years ago, I went on vacation to Europe. It hit me how useful it was knowing English. It came in handy in a lot of situations."

Step 4. Writing. On a separate sheet of paper, write a paragraph about a life-changing experience you have had.

Writing: Describe personality types

The paragraph

A paragraph consists of sentences about one topic. The most important sentence in a paragraph is the **topic sentence**. It is usually the first sentence, and it introduces the topic of a paragraph. For example:

Workaholics lead unbalanced lives.

In academic writing, all the **supporting sentences** that follow a topic sentence—details, examples, and other facts—must be related to the topic presented in the topic sentence.

The last sentence of the paragraph is often a **concluding sentence**. A concluding sentence restates the topic sentence or summarizes the paragraph. A concluding sentence often includes phrases such as <u>In conclusion</u> or <u>In summary</u>.

WRITING MODEL

Workaholics lead unbalanced lives. They spend all their energy on work. They rarely take time to relax and let their minds rest. I know because my father was a workaholic, and he worked every day of the week. We hardly ever saw him. Even when he was not at work, we knew he was thinking about work. He seemed never to think of anything else. In summary, not knowing how to escape from work makes it difficult for a workaholic to find balance in his or her life.

Step 1. Prewriting. Brainstorming ideas. Write a topic sentence for each personality type.

team players	tyrants	wise guys

1. ....

2. ....

3. ....

Now choose one of your topic sentences. On a separate sheet of paper, generate ideas you could use to support the topic.

Workaholics lead unbalanced lives.
—always think about work
—can't relax

Step 2. Writing. On a separate sheet of paper, write a paragraph about the personality type you chose in Step 1. Make sure all the supporting sentences relate to the topic. End with a concluding sentence.

Step 3. Self-Check.

☐ Does your paragraph have a topic sentence?
☐ Do the supporting sentences in your paragraph all relate to the topic?
☐ Do you have a concluding sentence?

SUMMIT WEBSITE
For Unit 1 online activities, visit the *Summit* Companion Website at www.longman.com/summit.

A 🎧 **Listening Comprehension.** Listen to the people talking about their reactions to events in the news. Decide if each speaker is an optimist, a pessimist, or a realist.

1. John .... **2.** Susan .... **3.** Matt ....

B Now read the statements. Write the name of the person from the listening who is most likely to have said each statement. Listen again if necessary.

1. "You've got to be practical. There will be some problems in life that you can solve and some that you can't. What's important is realizing when something is beyond your control. Then it's better just to move on." ....

2. "Life is full of hard times. You just have to accept the fact that bad things happen and know that there's very little you can do about it." ....

3. "It's important to see a problem as both a challenge to be faced and as an opportunity for success. Difficult experiences can make a person stronger." ....

C Complete each conversation with a personality type.

1. A: Looks like I have to work overtime again tonight. My supervisor just gave me three projects to complete by the end of the day.
B: You're kidding. He sounds like a real ....!

2. A: You know, without Sarah's help, I would never have completed that presentation in time.
B: Tell me about it. She really helped me out with my sales campaign last month. She's such a ....

3. A: Tom is really a .... I ran into him in the park last weekend, and he was sitting on a bench and working on that report.
B: Yeah, that's Tom all right. He never stops!

4. A: I don't think Jill had a very good time at the party—she didn't say a word the whole evening.
B: Well, Jill doesn't feel comfortable in social situations. She's just not a ....

5. A: Have you heard the news? My daughter Audrey got a perfect score on her entrance exam to law school.
B: Congratulations! I always knew she would do well in school. She's such a ....

6. A: I'm so tired of Ken. The other day I made a mistake at the computer lab at school, and he said something that really made me feel dumb.
B: Don't let it get to you. Everybody knows he's a .... Just try to ignore him.

D On a separate sheet of paper, write advice for each person. Use the verbs <u>stop</u>, <u>remember</u>, and <u>forget</u> with gerunds or infinitives.

She should stop working so much.

1. Samantha has a demanding job and works long hours. When she finally gets home, she's exhausted. She spends all weekend trying to catch up on housework and shopping.

2. Michael spends most of the day at the computer. Some days he doesn't even get outside except to walk to the bus stop. On the weekends, he just watches a lot of TV.

3. Philip is a single father with three kids, and he travels a lot for his company. He feels his kids are growing up so fast that he hardly ever sees them.

4. Marisa has been using her credit cards a lot lately, and she can't keep up with the monthly payments. And now she's having a hard time keeping up with *all* her bills.

UNIT 2

Musical Moods

PREVIEW

UNIT GOALS

1 Describe the music you listen to
2 Explain the role of music in your life
3 Describe a creative person
4 Discuss the benefits of music

A **Topic Preview.** Look at the reviews from the music website. Are you familiar with any of these artists?

TUNE IN 0 1 2 3 4 5 6 7 8 9 10

Artist ⬍ Go Search

Today's Picks

Home
New Releases
Explore by... genre instrument artist
Editor's Choice
Top Searches
Site Guide
Newsletter
About Us
Subscribe

LATIN

Carlos Ponce, *Ponce*
Puerto Rican singer / songwriter (and TV star) Carlos Ponce delivers a fun mix of romantic ballads and Caribbean-flavored dance grooves. Even if you don't understand Spanish, you can't help but feel the emotion in Ponce's voice, which ranges from a rough growl to a passionate cry.

JAZZ

Marcos Ariel, *My Only Passion*
Another brilliant set from the richly talented Brazilian keyboardist / composer Marcos Ariel. Check out the unpredictable interplay between the group members in "Bahia Suite," where Meia Noite's exciting percussion sets the tempo, while Ariel's piano races in and around Frank Gambale's surprising guitar lines.

POP

Andrea Bocelli, *Sogno*
Sogno finds the classically trained Bocelli moving away from the world of opera with a collection of modern pop ballads. Fans of Bocelli's remarkable voice won't be disappointed. Whether he's singing an Italian pop song or a lovely duet with pop diva Celine Dion, the depth and feeling of his music will touch your soul.

NEW AGE

Kitaro, *Best of Silk Road*
Described as "sound pictures" and "mind music" in his native Japan, Kitaro's electronic music incorporates the sounds of waves, wind, and rain, inspiring listeners to feel and appreciate the natural world. A true masterpiece.

URBAN DANCE

Beyoncé, *Dangerously in Love*
Beyoncé kicks off her solo career and keeps the dance floors crowded with her hit singles on this energetic recording. Hear the red-hot "Crazy in Love" (a duet with rap artist Jay-Z) and the playful "Baby Boy" (with dance-hall star Sean Paul) just once and you'll be humming them in your head all day.

WORLD

Muzsikás, *The Prisoner's Song*
Singing in Hungarian and playing traditional instruments, Muzsikás arranges ten Eastern European folk songs to tell a haunting story of love, desire, and freedom. Add lead singer Márta Sebestyén's amazing voice, and you've got a sound unlike any you've ever heard.

Source: www.allmusic.com

B **Discussion.**

1. Which reviews did you find the most appealing? Why? Which musical genres in the reviews interest you the most?
2. Can you think of other artists for each genre?

C 🎧 **Sound Bites.** Read and listen to a conversation between two friends comparing musical tastes.

TANIA: Wow! You've got quite a CD collection!

KEN: I guess so. Let's put something on.

TANIA: Got any jazz?

KEN: How about some Gato Barbieri? I've got *Fenix*.

TANIA: Actually, his saxophone playing kind of gets on my nerves on that one.

KEN: Really? I'm totally into him. *Fenix* is one of my all-time favorites.

TANIA: Yeah, but it's pretty hard to dance to.

KEN: Well, have you heard some of his later stuff?

TANIA: No, what's it like?

KEN: It's got more of a Latin feel. It'll definitely get the party started.

TANIA: Oh yeah? Let's give it a listen.

D **In Other Words.** Read the conversation again. With a partner, explain the meaning of each of the following statements or questions.

1. "You've got quite a CD collection."
2. "Let's put something on."
3. "His saxophone playing kind of gets on my nerves on that one."
4. "I'm totally into him."
5. "Have you heard some of his later stuff?"
6. "It'll definitely get the party started."
7. "Let's give it a listen."

STARTING **POINT**

What recordings are your all-time favorites? Complete the chart.

Title of recording	Artist or group	Genre of music

Pair Work. Talk with a partner about the music in your chart. Compare your musical tastes.

"I'm totally into Coldplay. That CD is fantastic!"

"Well, rock usually gets on my nerves, but maybe I'll give it a listen sometime."

1 *Describe the music you listen to*

Youssou N'Dour

A 🎧 CONVERSATION **SNAPSHOT**

A: So what have you been listening to lately?

B: Mostly world music. Ever heard of Youssou N'Dour?

A: I think so. He's from Senegal, right?

B: That's right.

A: You know, I've actually never heard his music. What's he like?

B: Well, he's got a terrific voice and a unique sound. I'd be happy to lend you a CD if you'd like.

A: All right, thanks. I'll let you know what I think.

🎧 **Rhythm and intonation practice**

B 🎧 **Vocabulary. Elements of music.** Listen and practice.

beat the rhythm of a piece of music
That song has a great beat you can dance to.

lyrics the words of a song
Her catchy lyrics make you want to sing along.

melody the order of notes in a musical piece
His song has an unforgettable melody.

sound the particular style or quality of an artist's or group's music
The band has created a new and exciting sound.

voice the quality of sound produced when one sings
She has a beautiful soprano voice.

C 🎧 **Pair Work.** Listen to the pieces of music. With a partner, use the words from the vocabulary to discuss what you like or don't like about the music.

Pronunciation Booster

PAGE P2
Intonation patterns

D Grammar. The present perfect and the present perfect continuous: finished and unfinished actions

Finished actions

Use the present perfect, not the present perfect continuous, when an action is completed at an unspecified time in the past. (Remember that actions completed at a specified time in the past require the simple past tense.)

I've already **heard** that CD. I heard it yesterday.
How many times **have** you **seen** Youssou N'Dour in concert?
I've **seen** him twice. As a matter of fact, I just saw him last week.

Very recently finished actions: an exception

The present perfect continuous is preferred to describe very recently completed actions when results can still be seen.

They've **been practicing**. I see them putting their instruments away.

Unfinished or continuing actions

Use the present perfect OR the present perfect continuous to describe actions that began in the past, continue into the present, and may continue into the future.

Have you **listened** to any jazz lately? OR **Have** you **been listening** to any jazz lately?
I've **listened** to Beethoven since I was a child. OR I've **been listening** to Beethoven since I was a child.

> **Words and phrases used with the present perfect for finished actions**
> already ever never yet
> once, twice, three times
> How many . . . ?

> **Words and expressions often used with unfinished actions**
> for   lately   these days
> since   recently   for a while
> all day   this year   How long . . . ?

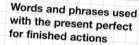

Grammar Booster

PAGE G3
For more . . .

CONVERSATION

E Read the sentences. Write <u>F</u> if the action is finished. Write <u>U</u> if the action is unfinished or continuing.

.... **1.** He's played with their band for almost ten years.

.... **2.** Caetano Veloso has made dozens of recordings.

.... **3.** They've never heard of Alexandre Pires.

.... **4.** We've been listening to that CD all day. Let's play something different.

.... **5.** Ladysmith Black Mambazo hasn't been playing many concerts lately.

.... **6.** Have you ever gone to a classical concert?

.... **7.** How many times have you heard Carmina Burana?

.... **8.** They've played Brahms's First Symphony twice this year.

F Complete the biography of Vanessa-Mae with the simple past tense, the present perfect, or the present perfect continuous. Use the present perfect continuous if the action is unfinished or continuing.

Vanessa-Mae .... music since she was a little girl.
(1. perform)
Born in Singapore on October 27, 1978, she .... her
(2. have)
first piano lesson at the age of three. A year later, she ....
(3. start)
taking violin lessons, and when she was just ten years old, she

.... her concert debut with the London Philharmonic.
(4. make)
Since then, Vanessa-Mae .... numerous classical
(5. make)
recordings, but it was in 1994 that she .... the field of
(6. enter)
pop music with *The Violin Player*. The album immediately .... extremely
(7. become)
popular with pop and classical music fans.

In more recent years, she .... with other pop artists such as Annie Lennox,
(8. play)
Janet Jackson, and Prince. Vanessa-Mae .... her audiences for over a decade,
(9. entertain)
and she continues to astonish them with her innovative sound.

Vanessa-Mae

CONVERSATION **STARTER** • *Now describe the music you listen to.*

Write some of the musical artists or bands you've been listening to lately.

Artist or band	What you like
Étoile de Dakar	*great dance beat*

Artist or band	What you like

Pair Work. Find out what your partner has been listening to lately. Ask what he or she likes or doesn't like about the music. Use the Conversation Snapshot on page 16 as a guide. Start like this: "So what have you been listening to lately?"

2 *Explain the role of music in your life*

A 🎧 GRAMMAR **SNAPSHOT.** Read the commentaries and notice the use of noun clauses.

Frankly, I can't imagine **what my life would be like without music**. It's **what gets me through the day**. Listening to music is **how I get going in the morning**. Later, at work, it's **how I stay productive**. And in the evening, it's **what helps me unwind**.

Patricia Nichols, 34
Vancouver, Canada

It's my opinion **that music is a kind of international language**—a way for people to communicate with **whomever they meet**. The fact **that enjoyment of music is universal** makes it an ideal way to bring cultures together. Music can open doors for you everywhere you go in the world.

Santigi Matomi, 27
Freetown, Sierra Leone

I'm a performer, and music is a part of who I am. It's a way for me to express **what's in my heart**. The truth is, **whether or not I perform** is not really a choice—I have to do it. **Whatever happens during the day**—good or bad—comes out in my music.

Alison Wu, 19
Shanghai, China

B **Discussion.** Do any of the comments above ring true for you? Why or why not?

C **Grammar.** **Noun clauses**

A noun clause can be a subject, a direct object, an indirect object, a subject complement, or the object of a preposition.

> **Whatever happens during the day** comes out in my music. [subject]
> I don't know **why I'm so crazy about his music**. [direct object]
> I'll give **whoever calls first** the tickets. [indirect object]
> Music is **what helps me unwind**. [subject complement]
> Music is a way for people to communicate with **whomever* they meet**.
> [object of a preposition]

Indirect speech is expressed using a noun clause.

> They asked **whether / if we could recommend some good recordings**.
> The violinist explained **that the concerto was quite difficult to play**.

A noun clause can also be introduced by whoever, whomever, or whatever, meaning any person or any thing.

> **Whoever can combine hip-hop with pop** is sure to be a hit.
> The audience always loves **whatever they play**.

Noun clauses often follow phrases with impersonal It subjects.

> It's my opinion **that music is a kind of international language**.

In writing, subject noun clauses are often preceded by phrases such as the fact, the idea, etc.

> The fact **that enjoyment of music is universal** is quite interesting.

*very formal

REMEMBER

A noun clause can begin with <u>that</u>, <u>if</u>, <u>whether (or not)</u>, or a question word.

> I believe **that** life would be empty without music.
> We asked them **if** they could play the song for us again.
> OR We asked them **whether (or not)** they could play the song for us again.
> I'm not sure **why** the band decided to break up.
> Do you know **which / what** instrument she plays?
> They asked her **how** she trained her voice to be so beautiful.

When a noun clause is a direct object, the word <u>that</u> may be omitted.

> I believe life would be empty without music.

BE CAREFUL! Use normal, not inverted, word order in noun clauses beginning with question words.

> NOT They asked her how ~~did she train~~ her voice to be so beautiful.

Grammar Booster

PAGE G4
For more …

D Introduce each noun clause with <u>that</u>, <u>if</u>, <u>whether (or not)</u>, or a question word.

Question words	
who	what
why	which
when	how
where	

1. It's his opinion .... classical music is boring.

2. Buying old records is .... I spend my Saturday afternoons.

3. I'm having difficulty recalling .... band played at the dance.

4. .... I like most is to take a hot bath while I listen to music.

5. Did they tell you .... the concert would start? I don't want to be late.

6. I can't really tell you .... I like some pieces of music. Maybe it's because they remind me of songs my mother sang to me when I was a child.

7. Robert asked me .... I had bought tickets yet.

8. She can't imagine .... she would do without music.

E Complete each statement with a noun clause that represents each question.

1. I don't know ....
   (Where did Mozart live?)

2. I have no idea ....
   (When did Georges Bizet compose *Carmen*?)

3. She told me ....
   (Where do the Black Sheep usually perform?)

4. I don't know ....
   (Which genre of music is his favorite?)

5. I'm not sure ....
   (What kind of lyrics does she write?)

GRAMMAR **EXCHANGE** • *Now explain the role of music in your life.*

Pair Work. Read the following quotations and underline the noun clauses. Classify each noun clause by its grammatical function within the sentence (subject, direct object, etc.). Then discuss the meaning of each quotation. Restate each in your own words.

"The audience knows when they're just listening to notes and when they're truly listening to music."
Sarah Chang, U.S. violinist
1980 –

"Music is a gift and a burden I've had since I can remember who I was."
Nina Simone, U.S. singer and pianist
1933 – 2003

"What I have in my heart must come out. This is why I compose music."
Ludwig van Beethoven, German composer
1770 – 1827

Discussion. Explain the role of music in your life. Do you listen to music at specific times during your day? What sorts of music do you listen to? Try to use noun clauses to explain your ideas.

Listening to music is . . .
I can't imagine . . .
It's my opinion . . .

3 Describe a creative person

A 🎧 **Vocabulary. Describing creative personalities.** Listen and practice.

Positive qualities

gifted having a natural ability to do one or more things extremely well
energetic very active, physically and mentally
imaginative able to think of new and interesting ideas
passionate showing a strong liking for something and being very dedicated to it

Negative qualities

eccentric behaving in an unusual way or appearing different from most people
difficult never satisfied and hard to please
moody quickly and easily becoming annoyed or unhappy
egotistical believing oneself to be better or more important than other people

B **Reading Warm-up.** It is often said that gifted people have eccentric or difficult personalities. Do you agree?

C 🎧 **Reading.** Read the short biography. What effect did Beethoven's personality have on his life?

Ludwig van Beethoven: *A Passion for Music*

*B*orn in 1770 in Bonn, Germany, Ludwig van Beethoven started playing the piano before he was four years old. By the time he was twelve, this child prodigy had already composed his first piece of music. When Beethoven was just sixteen, he went to study in Vienna, Austria, then the center of European cultural life and home to the most brilliant and passionate musicians and composers of the period. Beethoven proved to be a gifted pianist and an imaginative composer.

Beethoven is remembered for his great genius but also for his strong and difficult personality. In one infamous incident, Beethoven became so upset with a waiter that he emptied a plate of food over the man's head. Despite this type of behavior, many in musical and aristocratic circles admired Beethoven, and music lovers were always Beethoven's greatest supporters. This fact did not prevent him from losing his temper with one or another of them. However, because of his talent, Beethoven's friends always excused his insults and moody temperament.

Beethoven was also notorious for his eccentric behavior. He often walked through the streets of Vienna muttering to himself and stamping his feet. He completely neglected his personal appearance; his clothes would get so dirty that his friends would come and take them away during the night. When they replaced the old clothes with new ones, Beethoven never noticed the difference.

Although Beethoven was respected and admired by his audience, he was not concerned with pleasing them. Beethoven could play the piano so beautifully that some listeners cried; however, when he saw his fans crying, Beethoven only laughed and said they were fools. He was so egotistical that if people talked while he was performing, he would stop and walk away.

Beethoven wrote two famous works, *Moonlight Sonata* and *Für Elise*, for two different women he loved. He was almost always in love, often with a woman who was already married or engaged. Although Beethoven asked several women to marry him, they all rejected him. But the most tragic aspect of Beethoven's life was his gradual loss of hearing, beginning in his late twenties until he was completely deaf. However, even as his hearing grew worse, Beethoven continued to be energetic and productive; his creative activity remained intense, and audiences loved his music. In 1826, Beethoven held his last public performance of his famous Ninth Symphony. By this time, the maestro was completely deaf. When he was turned around so he could see the roaring applause that he could not hear, Beethoven began to cry.

Beethoven died in Vienna in 1827 at age fifty-seven. One out of ten people who lived in Vienna came to his funeral.

Source: www.classicalarchive.com

D **Pair Work.** Read each fact about Beethoven. Discuss which adjectives from the vocabulary you think best describe his behavior and actions. Complete the statements.

1. Beethoven was already publishing music and earning a salary at the age of twelve. He was very ....

2. Beethoven once told a prince, "There will be thousands of princes. There is only one Beethoven." He could be quite ....

3. Beethoven would work long hours composing and never seemed to tire. He was always .... when he performed for his audiences.

4. Beethoven had many close friends who tried to help him with his problems. He continually pushed them away and refused their assistance. He was considered to be a .... person.

5. Beethoven became frustrated when he began to lose his hearing. While socializing with his friends, he would often have sudden bursts of anger. He could be rather ....

6. Beethoven said that his music expressed what was inside of him and that he had no choice but to compose. He was a .... composer.

7. Beethoven's attention to feeling in his music began a new "style," different in some ways from Baroque music, which was popular at the time. His compositions were ....

8. Beethoven's friends thought he could be .... at times. For example, when he made coffee, he used to count out exactly sixty beans for each cup.

DISCUSSION **BUILDER** • *Now describe a creative person.*

Step 1. Pair Work. Rate your own personality on a scale of 0 to 3. Compare your answers with a partner's.

> *"I'm an extremely passionate person. I think it's really important to love what you do. What about you?"*

	0 = not at all	1 = a little	2 = somewhat	3 = extremely	
gifted ◯	eccentric ◯	passionate ◯	imaginative ◯	
difficult ◯	energetic ◯	moody ◯	egotistical ◯	creative ◯

Step 2. Discussion. Read the quotations from three famous musicians. Which one do you find the most interesting? After reading the quotations, how would you describe each musician's personality?

"Music is nothing separate from me. It is me. . . . You'd have to remove the music surgically."

Ray Charles, American soul singer, songwriter, and pianist, 1930 – 2004

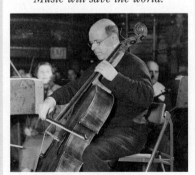

"Music will save the world."

Pablo Casals, Spanish cellist and conductor, 1876 – 1973

"I've outdone anyone you can name—Mozart, Beethoven, Bach, Strauss. Irving Berlin, he wrote 1,001 tunes. I wrote 5,500."

James Brown, American R & B singer and songwriter, 1933 –

Step 3. Writing. On a separate sheet of paper, write a brief biography of a creative person you know. Describe his or her personality. Explain how the person's creativity is related to his or her personality and achievements.

Discuss the benefits of music

A 🎧 **Listening Comprehension.** Read the questions. Then listen to Part 1 of a talk about an unusual use of music. Discuss the questions with a partner.

1. What does Dr. Schmidt do?

2. What sorts of people does she work with? Explain how she works with these people.

B 🎧 Read the questions. Then listen to Part 2 of the talk and answer the questions.

1. What are the four benefits Dr. Schmidt talks about?
   a. ....
   b. ....
   c. ....
   d. ....

2. What is one example of each?
   a. ....
   b. ....
   c. ....
   d. ....

C **Discussion.**

1. Can you think of any other benefits of music therapy?

2. Can you think of anyone who might benefit from music therapy? If so, how?

D Word Skills. Using participial adjectives

The present and past participle forms of many verbs function as adjectives.

The past participle has a passive meaning. Most sentences using past participles can be restated with a <u>by</u> phrase.

The patient is **depressed**. = The patient is depressed [by his life].
I'm **bored**. = I'm bored [by this movie].

The present participle does not have a passive meaning. Most sentences using present participles can be restated with an active verb.

That book is **depressing**. = That book depresses [everyone].
It's so **boring**. = It bores [me].

🎧 Present participles	Past participles
amazing	amazed
annoying	annoyed
boring	bored
depressing	depressed
disappointing	disappointed
entertaining	entertained
exciting	excited
interesting	interested
pleasing	pleased
relaxing	relaxed
soothing	soothed
stimulating	stimulated
touching	touched

E Circle the correct adjective to complete the sentence about music therapy.

1. Music can make patients feel (relaxed / relaxing).

2. Listening to music makes patients feel less (depressed / depressing).

3. Patients find some types of music to be very (soothed / soothing).

4. For patients in physical pain, the benefits of music can be (surprised / surprising).

5. Studies show that a student's ability to learn is (stimulated / stimulating) by music.

6. For patients with emotional problems, music can be very (comforted / comforting).

7. Many doctors report they are (pleased / pleasing) by the effect music has on their patients.

8. Many patients say that music therapy is (entertained / entertaining).

DISCUSSION **BUILDER** • *Now discuss the benefits of music.*

Step 1. Pair Work. What do you think are some benefits music brings to people's lives? Make a list and discuss.

Benefits

Music can be soothing.

Examples

Playing music at work can relax people so they're more productive.

Benefits

Examples

Step 2. Group Work. Present your ideas to the class. Comment on your classmates' ideas.

23

Writing: Describe yourself

Parallel structure

In a pair or a series, be sure to use parallel structure. All the words, phrases, or clauses should be in the same form.

Incorrect	Correct
He's a composer, singer, and a violinist. (article, no article, article)	He's **a** composer, **a** singer, and **a** violinist. (article, article, article) OR He's **a** composer, singer, and violinist. (one article for all three)
I like dancing, painting, and to sing. (gerund, gerund, infinitive)	I like **dancing, painting,** and **singing.** (gerund, gerund, gerund) OR I like **to dance, to paint,** and **to sing.** (infinitive, infinitive, infinitive) OR I like **to dance, paint,** and **sing.** (one <u>to</u> for all three)
The picture was framed, examined, and they sold it. (passive, passive, active)	The picture was **framed, examined,** and **sold.** (passive, passive, passive)

I like people who have the same interests as I do,
  make me laugh, or who like outdoor sports.
(clause, verb phrase, clause)
	I like people **who have the same interests as I do,**
	  who make me laugh, or **who like outdoor sports.**
	(clause, clause, clause)
	
	OR I like people who **have the same interests as**
	  I do, make me laugh, or **like outdoor sports.**
	(verb phrase, verb phrase, verb phrase)

Step 1. Prewriting. Clustering ideas.
Look at the idea cluster below. On a separate sheet of paper, create your own idea cluster. Draw a circle and write <u>ME</u> inside it. Then write any ideas that come to mind in circles around the main circle. Expand each new idea. Include hobbies, accomplishments, places you have traveled, interests, goals, etc.

Example

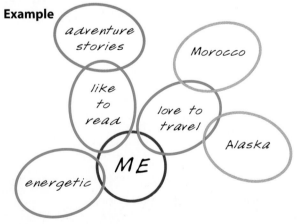

ERROR CORRECTION Correct the three errors.

I have always been a relaxed, passionate, and been a moody person. I love traveling, to meet new people, and learning about new places. I have been to many interesting places; for example, I have been on top of Mount Kilimanjaro, I have gone ice fishing with Eskimos in Alaska, and I rode on a camel in Morocco. These were some of

Step 2. Writing. On a separate sheet of paper, write a paragraph describing yourself, using the information from your cluster. Make sure to use parallel structure.

Step 3. Self-Check.

☐ Did you use parallel structure with pairs or series of nouns, adjectives, and adverbs?

☐ Did you use parallel structure with the clauses, phrases, and tenses?

☐ Does the topic sentence introduce the topic of the paragraph?

UNIT 2 CHECKPOINT

SUMMIT WEBSITE
For Unit 2 online activities, visit the
Summit Companion Website at
www.longman.com/summit.

A 🎧 **Listening Comprehension.** Listen to the conversations about musical preferences. Determine if each person likes the artist or group. Check the appropriate box or boxes. Then listen again and write what the person likes (voice, melody, lyrics, beat, or sound).

	the man	the woman	what he or she likes
1. Andrea Bocelli	☐	☐	....
2. Gato Barbieri	☐	☐	....
3. Ladysmith Black Mambazo	☐	☐	....
4. Beyoncé	☐	☐	....
5. Antonio Carlos Jobim	☐	☐	....

B Complete the statements with an appropriate adjective from the box.

eccentric	egotistical	energetic	gifted	moody	passionate

1. Sarah is a very .... musician. She started playing the piano when she was three.

2. My neighbor has thirty cats. You could say he's a bit ....

3. Franco is an extremely .... person. He only thinks of himself.

4. Dalia is so .... lately. She gets angry at the smallest thing.

C Circle the correct form of the verb to complete the paragraph.

Sandile Khemese (**1.** has played / played) the violin since he was a child in Johannesburg, South Africa. In 1989, Sandile (**2.** formed / has formed) the Soweto String Quartet with his brothers, Reuben and Thami, and their friend, Makhosini Mnguni. The group (**3.** played / has played) at President Nelson Mandela's inauguration in 1994. The Soweto String Quartet (**4.** won / has won) many music awards in South Africa, including Best New Artist. They (**5.** have recorded / have been recording) a number of successful CDs. In recent years, the Quartet (**6.** has been giving / gave) concerts all around the world.

D Underline the noun clause in each sentence. Write whether it is a subject, a direct object, a subject complement, or an object of a preposition.

1. I believe that without music life wouldn't be as much fun. ....

2. Whatever's playing on the radio is fine with me. ....

3. That's why Jorge likes only pop music. ....

4. Do you know where some good music is playing? ....

5. They'll listen to whatever music is playing. ....

UNIT 3

Money Matters

UNIT GOALS

1 Talk about your financial goals
2 Express buyer's remorse
3 Describe your spending habits
4 Discuss reasons for charitable giving

A **Topic Preview.** Read these financial tips.
Do you think you have a high financial IQ?

Three Tips for a High Financial IQ

1. Spend less than you earn.

The key to wealth is living below your means. If you make $300,000 a year and spend it all, you're not rich—you just have a lot of stuff. A job loss or serious illness could wipe you out in a few weeks. Your neighbors who make $50,000 and live on $40,000 are much wealthier. Fortunately, with today's technology, keeping a budget has never been easier. Invest in financial planning software that allows you to add up your income and expenses and keep a record of your spending.

2. Have a savings program.

Start saving early. If you invest $50 a week for 40 years and earn 9% interest, you will end up with $1,026,853. People spend because they get a good feeling from spending money. You can get that same good feeling from putting your money away in savings.

3. Pay off your credit cards.

Credit cards can be wonderful things. You can treat yourself to a spa retreat or a gourmet dinner without worrying whether you have the cash to pay for it. The downside, of course, is that credit cards let many people live beyond their means. So use credit cards, but pay the bill in full each month.

Source: *USA TODAY*, December 31, 1999. Reprinted with permission.

B **Discussion.** Which tip do you think is the most important one to follow? Why?
Can you think of any others?

C 🎧 **Sound Bites.** Read and listen to a conversation between two friends about saving money.

DAVID: Hey, a new entertainment system! What did you do—strike it rich?
JUDY: I wish! No, I saved up for it.
DAVID: There's no way I could do that. Too many bills.
JUDY: I know what you mean. My credit card bills used to be totally out of hand.
DAVID: Really? Then how did you manage to save up all that cash?
JUDY: Well, I just decided it was time to start living within my means. I cut way back on my spending.
DAVID: Wasn't that hard?
JUDY: Kind of. But I'm glad I did it.

a "piggy bank"

D **Pair Work.** Discuss the questions and explain your answers.

1. Do you think Judy makes a lot of money?
2. Do you think David is good with money?
3. What was Judy's financial situation like in the past?
4. What did Judy do to change her financial situation?
5. How would you describe Judy's financial IQ?
6. Are you more like Judy or David?

STARTING **POINT**

What's *your* financial IQ? Choose the statements that best apply to you.

1.	☐ I live within my means.	☐ I live beyond my means.
2.	☐ I keep track of my expenses.	☐ I don't know where the money goes.
3.	☐ I regularly put something away into savings.	☐ I spend everything I have and never save.
4.	☐ I always try to pay my credit card bills in full.	☐ I don't worry about paying my credit card bills off every month.
5.	☐ I always have enough money for what I need.	☐ I can't make ends meet!

Pair Work. Compare your answers with a partner's. Who do you think has the higher financial IQ?

1 Talk about your financial goals

A 🎧 GRAMMAR **SNAPSHOT.** Read the interview responses and notice how future plans are expressed.

What are your short-term and long-term financial goals?

I've decided to set a long-term goal for myself—to put aside enough money to buy a new car. **By this time next year,** I'll have put away enough cash for a down payment. My short-term goal is to start living within my means. **Once I've started** sticking to a monthly budget, I think it'll be easy.

David Michaels, 24
Brisbane, Australia

I find it really helps me to try and picture where I want to be over the next few years. **By next year,** I **hope to have gotten** a good job as a financial consultant. That's my short-term goal. My long-term goal? I **plan to have reached** real financial independence **before I retire.**

Su-jin Lee, 29
Wonju, Korea

My college expenses are going to get me into a lot of debt. I **don't expect to have begun** making payments **by the time I graduate,** but I do have a plan. After I finish school, my short-term goal is to find a job where I can make some good money and begin a payment plan on my loans. Then, I figure that **by the time I'm thirty,** I **should have paid** back everything I owe.

Robin Kraus, 22
Boston, USA

My long-term goal is **to have saved** enough money to spend a year traveling. **By the time I'm forty,** I'm sure I**'ll have saved** enough. **After I've seen** some of the world, I **plan to settle down** and buy a house.

Andreas Festring, 33
Munich, Germany

B **Discussion.** How similar are you to any of the people in the Grammar Snapshot? Do you share any of the goals they mentioned? If not, what are some of *your* goals?

C **Grammar.** Future plans and finished future actions

Future plans

Express general future plans with <u>expect</u>, <u>hope</u>, <u>intend</u>, or <u>plan</u> and an infinitive.
- We **hope to start** putting some money away.
- I **don't plan to be** financially dependent for the rest of my life.

Use the perfect form of an infinitive to express that an action will or might take place before a specified time in the future.
- By this time next year, I plan **to have saved up** enough cash to buy a new car.
- Her goal is **to have paid off** all her debt in five years.

Finished future actions

Use the future perfect to indicate an action that will be completed by a specified time in the future.
- By next year, I **will have completed** my studies, but I **won't have gotten** married.
- How much **will** you **have saved** by next month?

Use the present perfect in an adverbial clause to distinguish between a completed future action and one that will follow it.
- Once I**'ve completed** my studies, I'll get married.
- I'm going shopping when I**'ve finished** my report.

BE CAREFUL! Don't use the future perfect in the adverbial clause.
- NOT I'm going shopping when I ~~will have finished~~ my report.

Grammar Booster

PAGE G5
For more …

D Complete the paragraph about Ms. Kemper's future plans. Use <u>expect</u>, <u>hope</u>, <u>intend</u>, or <u>plan</u> and an infinitive form of the verb.

Jessica Kemper _____ business school this semester, and then she
　　　　　　　(1. complete)
_____ a job in the financial industry. However, Ms. Kemper has a lot of debt
(2. find)
to repay. She's borrowed some money from her parents and some from the bank, but she
_____ everyone back as soon as she can. She _____ a part-time job to
(3. pay)　　　　　　　　　　　　　　　　　　　　　(4. get)
help make ends meet while she's paying off her debt.

E Complete the paragraph about Mr. Randall's future plans. Use <u>expect</u>, <u>hope</u>, <u>intend</u>, or <u>plan</u> and a perfect form of the infinitive.

Paul Randall has been "drowning in debt," so he's decided to make some changes in his
financial habits. By the end of this month, he _____ a realistic budget that he can
　　　　　　　　　　　　　　　　　　　　　　　　　　(1. create)
follow. As a matter of fact, he _____ one of his last credit cards by October.
　　　　　　　　　　　　　　(2. pay off)
In addition, he _____ putting some money away in savings. If he can stick to his
　　　　　　　(3. begin)
budget, he _____ most of his debt within the year.
　　　　　　(4. pay back)

F On a separate sheet of paper, use the cues to write sentences with the future perfect.

1. By the end of this month / I / put 10 percent of my paycheck in the bank.
2. By the summer / I / save enough to go to Italy.
3. you / pay off your credit card balance by December?
4. When / they / pay the bill in full?

Pronunciation Booster
PAGE P3
Sentence rhythm

GRAMMAR **EXCHANGE** • *Now talk about your financial goals.*

Write your short-term and long-term financial goals on your notepad.

IDEAS
- be financially independent
- save enough to buy _____
- cut back on expenses
- create a budget
- pay my debts in full
- live within my means

short-term goals	completion dates	long-term goals	completion dates
buy a new car	by this time next year	buy a house	by the time I'm thirty

short-term goals	completion dates	long-term goals	completion dates

Pair Work. Describe your future financial goals to your partner.

"Once I've started working, I plan to put a little something into savings every week."

"By the time I graduate, I hope to have saved enough to buy a new car."

29

2 *Express buyer's remorse*

A 🎧 CONVERSATION **SNAPSHOT**

A: Hey, I heard you got an E-tec MP3 player. Lucky you!

B: Well, to tell you the truth, I could kick myself.

A: What do you mean?

B: I had no idea it would be so hard to operate.
It took me hours to figure out how to download a song.

A: What a pain!

B: You're telling me. Had I known, I would have gotten a
different brand.

🎧 **Rhythm and intonation practice**

B 🎧 Vocabulary. **Expressing buyer's remorse.** Listen and practice.

It costs so much to maintain.

It takes up so much room.

It's so hard to operate.

It's so hard to put together.

It just sits around collecting dust.

C 🎧 Listening Comprehension. Listen to the conversations in which people regret having bought something. Complete each statement by inferring the reason for buyer's remorse.

1. He's sorry he bought it because ....
   a. it costs so much to maintain   **b.** it takes up so much room

2. She's sorry she bought it because ....
   a. it's so hard to operate   **b.** it's so hard to put together

3. She's sorry she bought it because ....
   a. it takes up so much room   **b.** it just sits around collecting dust

4. He's sorry he bought it because ....
   a. it just sits around collecting dust   **b.** it's so hard to put together

5. She's sorry she bought it because ....
   a. it costs so much to maintain   **b.** it's so hard to operate

D **Grammar.** **The past unreal conditional: inverted form**

Past unreal conditionals can be stated without **if**. Invert **had** and the subject.

If I had known it would take up so much room, I wouldn't have bought it.	→	**Had I known** it would take up so much room, I wouldn't have bought it.
I might have gotten another brand **if I had realized** it would be so hard to operate.	→	I might have gotten another brand **had I realized** it would be so hard to operate.
If we hadn't been so busy, we could have shopped around.	→	**Had we not been** so busy, we could have shopped around.
If I'd been told they wouldn't operate without batteries, I would never have considered getting them.	→	**Had I been told** they wouldn't operate without batteries, I would never have considered getting them.

REMEMBER

Use the past unreal conditional to describe unreal or untrue conditions and results.

E On a separate sheet of paper, rewrite the following past unreal conditional sentences, using the inverted form.

1. They would have lent her the money if she had asked.

2. If I had been debt free, I would have considered buying that house.

3. If the Carsons hadn't been able to support their son, he would have had to find a part-time job.

4. Could you have gotten the car if they hadn't raised the price?

F **Pair Work.** Make statements of buyer's remorse, using the inverted form of the past unreal conditional and the vocabulary.

1. . . . I would never have gotten that espresso maker.

2. . . . we never would have bought such a large sofa.

3. . . . I could have gotten an entertainment center with fewer pieces.

4. . . . we probably would have bought a more economical car.

5. . . . I would have gotten a DVD player with simpler directions.

"Had I known it would take up so much room, I would never have gotten that espresso maker."

CONVERSATION **STARTER** • *Now express buyer's remorse.*

Pair Work. On your notepad, answer the questions about something *you* regret buying. Tell your partner about it.

Role Play. Role-play a conversation about the item on your notepad. Use the Conversation Snapshot on page 30 as a guide. Start like this: "Hey, I heard you got . . . ."

What did you buy?

Why did you buy it?

Do you still have it?

If so, where is it?

If not, what did you do with it?

Would you ever buy a similar item again?

Why or why not?

3

"Money Talks" *with Lara Savino*

Describe your spending habits

A 🎧 **Listening Comprehension.** Read the statements. Then listen to a radio call-in show and check <u>True</u> or <u>False</u>.

	True	False
1. Steve finds it hard to save money.	☐	☐
2. Steve buys a lot on credit.	☐	☐
3. Steve spends less money than he makes.	☐	☐
4. Steve has been on a budget for three months.	☐	☐

B 🎧 Now listen again. What are the three tips Lara Savino gives the caller?

1. ....

2. ....

3. ....

C **Discussion.**

1. Why do you think Steve has a problem with money?

2. Which tip do you think is the most useful? Why?

D 🎧 **Vocabulary. Describing spending habits.** Listen and practice.

<table>
<tr><td rowspan="3">NOUNS</td><td>a big spender someone who likes to spend large amounts of money</td><td rowspan="3">ADJECTIVES</td><td>generous willing to give more money, time, etc., than is expected</td></tr>
<tr><td>a spendthrift someone who spends money carelessly, especially when he or she doesn't have a lot of it</td><td>cheap / stingy unwilling to spend or give money, even when one has a lot of it</td></tr>
<tr><td>a cheapskate / a tightwad someone who does not like spending money and can be unpleasant about it</td><td>thrifty / frugal using money carefully and wisely</td></tr>
</table>

E Complete the sentences about people's spending habits.

1. Can you believe what .... Martin is! He refused to leave a tip for the waiter!

2. Our grandmother donates to many organizations. She's always been very .... with her money.

3. He's so .... that he wouldn't even lend his own son money.

4. George must be wealthy. He's such .... He always insists on treating his friends to dinner.

5. If you try to be more .... with your money, you'll have enough when you really need it.

6. Unless you stop being such ...., you're going to get deeper in debt.

LISTENING

Step 1. Pair Work. First circle the letter that best completes the statement for you. Then compare your answers with a partner's. Find out if your spending habits are the same or different.

Spending Habits Self-Test

1. You hear a great new song on the radio. You . . .

A. buy the CD at the first store you find it in.
B. shop around until you find the CD on sale.
C. borrow it from a friend.
D. other: ....

2. You'd love a state-of-the-art big-screen TV but you just don't have the money right now. You . . .

A. use your credit card and hope you get a raise this year.
B. cut back on other expenses until you've saved enough.
C. wait until big-screen TVs come down in price.
D. other: ....

3. You have lunch with your two best friends. Your meal was cheaper than theirs. When the bill comes, you . . .

A. offer to pay the entire bill.
B. suggest splitting the bill equally.
C. pay only what you owe.
D. other: ....

4. You're invited to a wedding. You . . .

A. spend more on a gift than you can afford.
B. spend as little on a gift as you can.
C. don't go so you don't have to buy a gift.
D. other: ....

5. You discover a hole in your favorite jacket. You . . .

A. go out and buy a new jacket.
B. have the jacket repaired.
C. wear the jacket—it's no big deal.
D. other: ....

Count up your score.

If you circled three or more As:
You can be generous at times, but you're a bit of a spendthrift. Your motto is "**Easy come, easy go!**"

If you circled three or more Bs:
You're usually very careful with your money—even thrifty. Your motto is "**Everything in moderation.**"

If you circled three or more Cs:
You hate spending money. Some might say you're a tightwad. Your motto is "**Money doesn't grow on trees!**"

If you circled three or more Ds:
How would *you* describe your spending habits?

Step 2. Group Work. Tell your classmates about your spending habits or your partner's.

Step 3. Writing. On a separate sheet of paper, describe your spending habits.

I make a good living, but I have trouble sticking to a budget and

4 *Discuss reasons for charitable giving*

A 🎧 **Vocabulary. Charity and investment.** Listen and practice.

char·i·ty /ˈtʃærəti/ *n. plural* **charities 1** [C] an organization that gives money, goods, or help to people who are poor, sick etc. **2** [U] charity organizations in general

con·tri·bu·tion /ˌkɑntrəˈbyuʃən/ *n.* **1** [C] something that you give or do in order to help something be successful **2** [C] an amount of money that you give in order to help pay for something

in·vest·ment /ɪnˈvɛstmənt/ *n.* **1** [C,U] the money that people or organizations have put into a company, business, or bank, in order to get a profit or to make a business activity successful **2** [C,U] a large amount of time, energy, emotion etc. that you spend on something

phi·lan·thro·pist /fɪˈlænθrəpɪst/ *n.* [C] a rich person who gives money to help people who are poor or who need money to do useful things

pro·fit /ˈprɑfɪt/ *n.* [C,U] money that you gain by selling things or doing business

Excerpted from *Longman Advanced American Dictionary* © 2005

B **Reading Warm-up.** What are some reasons people donate money? What kinds of people or organizations get contributions? Why?

C 🎧 **Reading.** Read the article. What reasons does Paul Newman give for donating to charity?

Paul Newman: Actor and Philanthropist

Paul Newman has been acting since 1954 and has appeared in more than fifty films. He won an Oscar for best actor in 1986 for *The Color of Money*. In 1993, Newman received a special Oscar for humanitarian service. These two awards reflect his dual success as actor and philanthropist.

In 1982, Newman and a friend, A. E. Hotchner, founded Newman's Own, a not-for-profit food products company. The company's first product was a salad dressing that Newman and Hotchner made at home themselves. Newman was told that the salad dressing would sell only if his face were on the label. Though he didn't want to call attention to himself, Newman agreed because he planned to donate all profits to charity. The salad dressing was a big success: In the first year, Newman contributed approximately US $1,000,000 to charitable organizations.

Newman's Own has expanded, and the company now makes many other food products. Every year, Newman donates 100 percent of the profits from the sale of Newman's Own products to thousands of educational and charitable organizations located in the United States, Japan, France, Brazil, and Australia. Since 1982, Newman has made contributions of more than US $150 million to charities.

One of Newman's special projects is the Hole in the Wall Gang Camps, the world's only network of camps for children with life-threatening illnesses. At these camps, children participate in many outdoor activities where they can temporarily forget their illnesses. Newman and other generous donors have sponsored over 70,000 children to attend these camps free of charge. When asked why he gives so much to children with illnesses, Newman says, "I've had such a string of good fortune in my life…. Those who are most lucky should hold their hands out to those who aren't."

Paul Newman doesn't think that being philanthropic is an exceptional quality. To him, generosity is simply a human trait, a common-sense way of living. "I respect generosity in people. I don't look at it as philanthropy. I see it as an investment in the community. I am not a professional philanthropist," says Newman. "I'm not running for sainthood. I just happen to think that in life we need to be a little like the farmer who puts back into the soil what he takes out."

*"I don't look at it as philanthropy.
I see it as an investment in the community."*

Source: www.newmansown.com

D **Discussion.**

1. Why do you think Paul Newman's face has helped to sell his products?

2. Do you think that the work Newman is doing is making a difference?

3. In your opinion, do famous or wealthy people have a responsibility to "give back" or to share what they have with others?

DISCUSSION **BUILDER** • *Now discuss reasons for charitable giving.*

Step 1. Pair Work. Read the list of possible reasons some people donate money. In your opinion, which are good reasons? Explain.

- to change society
- to feel good about themselves
- to get publicity or advertising
- to say "thank you" for past help
- to share what they have with others

- to give new opportunities to people
- to satisfy religious beliefs
- so other people will thank them
- so other people will admire them
- other: ....

Step 2. On your notepad, check the people or organizations to whom you might consider making a contribution. List your reasons for giving or *not* giving.

People / Organizations	Reasons for giving or *not* giving
☐ a homeless person	
☐ a seriously ill person	
☐ a political candidate	
☐ a disaster relief agency	
☐ a hospital	
☐ a school in a poor neighborhood	
☐ a theater or a museum	
☐ a local charity	
☐ an international charity	
☐ a religious institution	
☐ other:	

Step 3. Discussion. Talk about the people and organizations you would or would not give money to. Explain your reasons.

> *"I would rather give money to a local charity because they'll use it to help people in my community."*

Step 4. Writing. Choose one person, charity, or type of organization people donate money to. On a separate sheet of paper, write a paragraph explaining the reasons people have for or against donating.

Writing: Explain your financial goals

Sequencing events

When writing a paragraph, the sentences need to be logically organized. **Time order words** are used to clarify the order of events in someone's life, to present the steps in a process, or to give instructions.

Special time order words and expressions help make sequence clear:

- First,
  First of all,
  To begin with,

- Second,
  Third,

- Next,
  Then,

- After,
  Afterwards,
  After that,

- Finally,
  Lastly,
  In the end,

WRITING MODEL

I intend to be financially independent by the time I am sixty. How? **First,** I plan to live within my means. I will cut corners where I can and stick to my budget. **Then,** I hope to open up my own business. **Next,** I intend to start putting some money away. **After that,** I plan to make some smart investments. **Finally,** by the time I am sixty, I will have saved up enough to retire and buy a nice weekend house.

Topics
- My long-term financial goals
- The steps I need to take in order to buy ....

Step 1. Prewriting. Listing ideas. Choose a topic. Then complete the chart.

Topic: ....

	Goal or step	My plan	Completion date
First,			
Then,			
After that,			
Finally,			

Step 2. Writing. Write a paragraph, using your notes. Use time order words and expressions to organize the sequence of goals or steps in your paragraph. Remember to write a topic sentence.

Step 3. Self-Check.

☐ Did you use time order words or expressions in the paragraph?

☐ Does the sequence of events in the paragraph make sense?

☐ Does the topic sentence introduce the topic of the paragraph?

SUMMIT **WEBSITE**
for Unit 3 online activities, visit the *Summit* Companion Website at
www.longman.com/summit.

A 🎧 **Listening Comprehension.** Listen to the conversations about money matters. Then decide which statement best summarizes each conversation. Listen again if necessary.

Conversation 1. .... **Conversation 2.** .... **Conversation 3.** ....

   a. If he'd known it would just sit around collecting dust, he never would have bought it.

   b. He's too much of a spendthrift. He should be more frugal.

   c. He's not a spendthrift. He's just feeling generous.

   d. If he'd known it would be so hard to put together, he never would have bought it.

B Complete the statements with words from the box.

   1. Steve Gold, an assistant to a big executive at World Corp, saved his company a lot of money by purchasing airplane tickets online from a discount travel website. His boss appreciated his being so ....

   2. Bill Gates, founder of the Microsoft Corporation, is not only one of the richest men in the world, but he's also one of the most .... Since 2000, he has donated over US$7.5 billion to improve global health and education.

   3. Dan Fielding expected that his .... in the ComTech Corporation would result in a nice .... However, the business failed and Dan lost all of his money.

   4. One of the richest women in history, Hetty Green was also notoriously .... She once refused to light the candles on her birthday cake so she could return them to the store for a refund. Hetty is considered to be history's greatest ....

   5. Andrew Carnegie was a famous .... who gave away over US$350 million to .... His largest .... was for US$56 million dollars, which was used to build over 2,500 free public libraries around the world.

charities
contribution
frugal
generous
investment
philanthropist
profit
stingy
tightwad

C Write a conditional sentence for each regret below. Begin with an inverted form ("Had I ...").

   1. a regret about your financial situation

   ....

   2. a regret about something you bought

   ....

   3. a regret about a relationship

   ....

D Express your future plans and goals. Use the perfect form of an infinitive or the future perfect.

   1. Before the end of today, I plan ....

   2. By next month, I will ....

   3. By the end of this English course, I expect ....

   4. By the end of the year, I intend ....

   5. Within five years, I hope ....

UNIT 4

Looking Good

UNIT GOALS

1 Discuss appropriate dress
2 Comment on fashion and style
3 Evaluate ways to change one's appearance
4 Describe what makes a person beautiful

A **Topic Preview.** These pictures depict concepts of ideal beauty at different times and in different places. Do *you* find any of these fashions attractive?

For centuries in Japan, the geisha defined beauty and grace.

In eighteenth-century Europe, well-to-do men and women wore extravagant wigs and clothing.

In India, Pakistan, the Middle East, and Africa, women paint their faces and hands with henna for special occasions.

Paduang women of Myanmar begin lengthening their necks with gold bands at the age of five or six.

In New Zealand, it is traditional for Maori men to decorate their faces and bodies with tattoos.

B **Discussion.**

1. What things do people do today to make themselves more attractive? Which techniques do you think are the most successful?

2. In your opinion, why do tastes change over time from culture to culture?

3. What do you think this expression means? Do you agree?

*Beauty is in the eye of the beholder.**

*beholder—the person who is looking

C 🎧 **Sound Bites.** Read and listen to a conversation between a couple about dressing up and dressing down.

MARGO: Don't you think you might be a little overdressed?

PAUL: What do you mean?

MARGO: Hello! The invitation said casual.

PAUL: Oops. I thought we were supposed to get dressed up. Be right back.

PAUL: How's this?

MARGO: Now that's a little *too* casual.

PAUL: Margo! I wish you'd make up your mind.

MARGO: And what's with the baggy pants?

PAUL: OK. If I change into a polo shirt and a pair of slacks, will that work?

MARGO: Perfect.

D **Pair Work.** Use the following words to tell the story of what happened in the conversation.

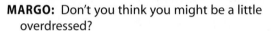

| underdressed | overdressed | formal | casual |

STARTING **POINT**

Pair Work. Look at the pictures. Are the people dressed appropriately for each event? With a partner, use the words from Exercise D to describe how the people are dressed. Then compare your answers with other students'.

Event:
a company picnic

Event:
an outdoor wedding

Event:
a dinner party at a friend's home

Event:
English class

Discussion.

1. When was the last time you got dressed up? What did you wear?

2. Have you ever been underdressed or overdressed for an event? What happened? How did you feel?

39

1 *Discuss appropriate dress*

A 🎧 GRAMMAR **SNAPSHOT.** Read the article and notice the use of quantifiers.

Dressing Up for Work

Formal business attire: a thing of the past?

Most professionals around the world wear formal business attire to work in company offices. In **many** countries, there is an unwritten dress code making it mandatory for a man to wear a dark suit and tie and for a woman to wear a skirted suit. But in **several** countries, **more** companies are experimenting with casual business dress during working hours.

In Australia, during the hotter summer months, **a number of** companies are allowing employees to leave their suits at home. And in the United States, **a little over half of all** office workers are allowed to dress down on Fridays. **One third of** U.S. companies make the standard business suit optional—allowing casual clothing **every** day. There is **a great deal of** interest in a casual dress code because of its attraction to new employees.

However, **some** critics complain that casual dress in the office causes **a lot of** problems, among them, **less** productivity. **Each** manager needs to decide if "business casual" is right for his or her company. **A few** experts in the fashion industry claim that the trend toward casual office dress is on the way out. But a recent survey found that **a majority of** employees say their company dress code is at least as casual or more casual than it was two years ago.

Some complain that business casual leads to less productivity.

B **Discussion.**

1. How do professionals dress for work in your country? Do people ever wear "business casual"? What kinds of clothing are mandatory?

2. Do you think the way a person dresses has an effect on how he or she works? In what way?

C **Grammar. Quantifiers**

Some quantifiers can only be used with singular count nouns.

one person	**each** manager	**every** employee

Some quantifiers can only be used with plural count nouns.

two problems	**a couple of** employees	**both** companies
a few managers	**a number of** businesses	**several** women
many young people	**a majority of** professionals	

Some quantifiers can only be used with non-count nouns.

a little conformity	**much** choice	**a great deal of** interest
less productivity	**not as much** satisfaction	

Some quantifiers can be used with *both* count and non-count nouns.

no people	**no** choice
some / any employees	**some / any** conformity
a lot of / lots of companies	**a lot of / lots of** individuality
a third of the companies	**a third of** the money
plenty of businesses	**plenty of** satisfaction
most managers	**most** dissatisfaction
all young people	**all** innovation
more countries	**more** interest

> **NOTE:** The quantifier <u>a majority of</u> can also be used with singular count nouns that include more than one person. Use a third-person singular verb.
>
> A majority of **the class thinks** business casual is a good idea.
>
> A majority of **the population prefers** a strict dress code.

PAGE G6
For more …

D Circle the correct quantifier.

1. (Most / Much) businesspeople today prefer to dress casually.

2. (A number of / A great deal of) companies would prefer not to change their dress codes.

3. (All / Every) manager has to decide what is best for the company and its employees.

4. (One / Several) company in New Zealand decided to try a "casual summer" because the summers are always so hot.

5. Research has shown that a business casual dress code has resulted in (less / a few) job dissatisfaction among professionals.

6. (A little / A few) companies are returning to a more formal dress code.

E **Pair Work.** Read the Grammar Snapshot again. On a separate sheet of paper, rewrite the article, using different quantifiers with similar meanings.

> **M**ost professionals around the world wear formal business attire to work in company offices.

> *A majority of professionals around the world wear formal business attire to work in company offices.*

F 🎧 **Listening Comprehension.** Listen to the conversations about casual and formal dress. Determine how best to complete each statement.

1. He'd prefer to ....   **a.** dress up   **b.** dress down
2. She wants to ....   **a.** dress up   **b.** dress down
3. He's pretty sure a tie is .... **a.** optional   **b.** mandatory
4. She thinks a dress is ....   **a.** optional   **b.** mandatory

GRAMMAR **EXCHANGE** • *Now discuss appropriate dress.*

Pair Work. How do you think people in your country would generally suggest dressing for these events? Discuss appropriate and inappropriate dress for each event.

> *"Most people would ...,
> but a few people ...."*

Events
- a business meeting
- dinner at a nice restaurant
- dinner at the home of your friend's parents
- an evening party at a club or restaurant with your classmates
- an in-class party

Group Work. Compare your classmates' opinions. Use quantifiers to summarize your classmates' ideas.

> *"A majority of the class said ...."*

> *"A few students said ...."*

Discussion.

1. Do you think it's important to dress according to social conventions?

2. How does what people wear affect how others perceive them?

CONVERSATION

Comment on fashion and style

A 🎧 CONVERSATION **SNAPSHOT**

A: Check out that guy over there.

B: Which guy?

A: The one on the cell phone. Can you believe what he's wearing?

B: What do you mean?

A: Don't you think that shirt's a little flashy?

B: Well, the colors are pretty loud, but that's what's in style.

🎧 **Rhythm and intonation practice**

B 🎧 **Vocabulary. Describing fashion and style.**
Listen and practice.

Attractive

fashionable / stylish
in style / trendy / hot*
elegant / chic
striking

modern
temporarily popular
in good taste
attention-getting

Unattractive

old-fashioned / out of style
tacky*
flashy*
shocking

no longer popular
in poor taste
attention-getting
offensive

*informal

Pronunciation Booster

PAGE P3
Linking sounds

C 🎧 **Listening Comprehension.** Listen to the conversations about fashion and style. Choose the adjective that best summarizes each speaker's point of view.

1. They think the purses in the magazine are ....
   a. hot   **b.** flashy   **c.** elegant

2. He thinks the jacket Carl is wearing is ....
   a. stylish   **b.** flashy   **c.** striking

3. They think the girl's hairstyle is ....
   a. striking   **b.** old-fashioned   **c.** shocking

4. He thinks the dress the salesperson is suggesting is ....
   a. elegant   **b.** striking   **c.** trendy

5. She thinks the blouse her friend's holding is ....
   a. out of style   **b.** tacky   **c.** chic

D **Discussion.** What do you think of these fashions and hairstyles? Use the adjectives from the vocabulary to describe them in your *own* way.

E **Pair Work.** Read and match each quote with a person in the photos in Exercise D. Explain your answers. Which quote sounds the most like *you*?

1. ◯ *"Clothing should express your individuality. I don't want to conform to how other people look or what they wear—I prefer to stand out in a crowd."*

4. ◯ *"I draw the line at wild and crazy clothes. I just don't like to attract attention to myself. I'm a lot more comfortable in subdued colors and classic styles."*

2. ◯ *"What I wear may not be the most trendy— but I like it that way. I'd rather be comfortable than fashionable."*

5. ◯ *"I prefer a look that isn't just a fad that won't be in style for very long. I prefer clothes that are well made—they may cost a bit more, but they last longer."*

3. ◯ *"The way you dress affects how people perceive you, so it's important to dress well. I always choose designer labels—they're the best."*

CONVERSATION **STARTER** • *Now comment on fashion and style.*

Complete each statement about fashions in your *own* way.
Use these words and expressions.

I prefer clothes that . . .
I don't like to . . .
I dislike it when women wear clothes that . . .
I dislike it when men wear clothes that . . .

conform
stand out
attract attention
express one's
  individuality

old-fashioned
out of style
tacky
flashy
shocking

well made
comfortable
wild and crazy
classic
subdued
fashionable
stylish
elegant
striking
trendy

Pair Work. Discuss your *own* fashion tastes and style. Explain why you find some fashions attractive and some unattractive. Refer to the photos on this page or bring in others. Use the Conversation Snapshot on page 42 as a guide.

"Check out . . ."   *"Can you believe . . ."*

3 *Evaluate ways to change one's appearance*

A 🎧 **Listening Comprehension.** Listen to Part 1 of a radio program about men's hairstyles. Then read the statements and listen again. Complete the statements, according to the information in the program.

1. In the eighteenth century, wigs were considered ....
   a. chic **b.** tacky **c.** out of style

2. In the nineteenth century, wigs were considered ....
   a. in style **b.** old-fashioned **c.** striking

3. Before the twentieth century, short hair would not have been considered ....
   a. stylish **b.** out of style **c.** shocking

a goatee

B 🎧 Now listen to Part 2. What generally happened to men's hairstyles in the mid-twentieth century?

C 🎧 Read the following statements and listen to Part 2 again. Complete the statements, according to the information in the program.

1. Men changed their hairstyles in the 1960s as a .... statement.
   a. fashion **b.** social and political **c.** religious and moral

2. Twenty years ago, the bald look would have been considered ....
   a. eccentric **b.** stylish **c.** old-fashioned

3. Young people who dye their hair want to ....
   a. be stylish **b.** conform **c.** express their individuality

D **Discussion.** Do you agree with the hair stylist that "anything goes" today for men's hairstyles? Are there any hairstyles that you really don't like on a man? Do you think men's hairstyles have improved or gotten worse in recent times?

sideburns

highlights

long hair

a buzz cut

bald

dyed

braids

DISCUSSION **BUILDER** • *Now evaluate ways to change one's appearance.*

Step 1. Pair Work. Discuss and complete the checklist.

Ways people spend time and money to make themselves more attractive

Which do you think are good ideas for women? How about for men? Which do you think are good for both? Check the appropriate box.

	men	women		men	women
skin lightening	☐	☐	contact lenses	☐	☐
skin tanning	☐	☐	false eyelashes	☐	☐
body piercing	☐	☐	makeup	☐	☐
tattoos	☐	☐	hair coloring	☐	☐
facials	☐	☐	permanents (perms)	☐	☐
manicures	☐	☐	hair transplants	☐	☐
nail extensions	☐	☐	wigs	☐	☐
nail polishing	☐	☐	hair removal	☐	☐
cosmetic surgery	☐	☐	other	☐	☐

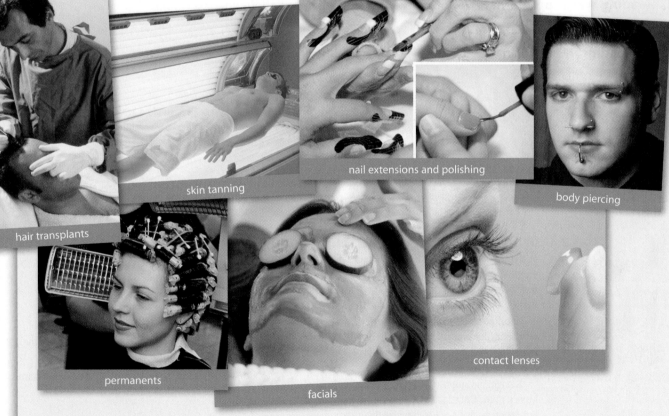

hair transplants

skin tanning

nail extensions and polishing

body piercing

permanents

facials

contact lenses

Step 2. Discussion.

1. Who do you think should spend more time making themselves attractive— men or women? Why?

2. Can people do too much to try to make themselves attractive? If so, what do you think is "too much"?

Describe what makes a person beautiful

A 🎧 **Word Skills. Using the prefix self-.** Use a dictionary to find other words with the prefix self-.

NOUNS

self-confidence the belief that one has the ability to do things well
Parents can build their children's self-confidence by praising their accomplishments.

self-esteem the attitude of acceptance and approval of oneself
High self-esteem can help a person succeed, and low self-esteem can be damaging.

self-image the opinion one has about one's own abilities, appearance, and character
Mark's self-image improved after he started his new job.

self-pity the feeling of being sorry for oneself
It's easy to indulge in self-pity when you're faced with problems.

ADJECTIVES

self-centered interested only in oneself
Children are naturally self-centered, but they usually learn to be more interested in others as they grow up.

self-confident sure of oneself; not shy or nervous in social situations
Janet is a very self-confident young woman. She'll do well at the university.

self-conscious worried about what one looks like or what other people think of one's appearance
Everyone at the meeting was dressed casually, so I felt self-conscious in my suit.

self-critical tending to find fault with oneself
Paul is too self-critical. He always focuses on his mistakes rather than his accomplishments.

B **Reading Warm-up.** Do you think most people are self-conscious about how they look?

C 🎧 **Reading.** Read the article about female body image. What do you think is expressed in the song lyrics?

The average fashion model is 5 feet, 11 inches (1.83 meters) tall and weighs 117 pounds (53 kilograms). The average woman is 5 feet, 4 inches (1.65 meters) tall and weighs 140 pounds (63.5 kilograms).

WHO DEFINES BEAUTY?

*"Am I not pretty enough?
Is my heart too broken?
Do I cry too much?
Am I too outspoken?
Don't I make you laugh?
Should I try it harder?
Why do you see right through me?"*

What makes a girl beautiful? The lines above are from the song "Not Pretty Enough," written and performed by Kasey Chambers, an Australian folk-rock singer and songwriter. The words tell us a lot about what it's like to be female in a society in which media such as television, movies, and magazines define what it means to be beautiful.

In cultures where success and happiness are equated with being thin and attractive "just like models or movie stars," many young women are left feeling either invisible or fat and unaccepted.

It might not surprise you to read that 75 percent of women in the United States think that they are "too fat." But many people do not realize how these ideas about body image have affected teenagers and children. You don't have to look much farther than a billboard sign, magazine advertisement, or popular television show to see how girls and women are being presented and to understand how it affects them.

On average, U.S. children age eight or older spend almost seven hours a day watching television, playing video games, or reading magazines. Studies have revealed these trends:

- If they had just one wish, girls ages eleven to seventeen say they would wish to be thinner.
- Between the ages of ten and fourteen, the percentage of girls who are "happy with the way I am" drops from 60% to 29%.
- 80% of ten-year-old girls are on diets.
- Between 5 and 10 million teenage girls and young women have an eating disorder—extreme dieting—that can be dangerous to their health.
- Teenage cosmetic surgeries more than doubled in the last decade and are growing at an alarming rate.
- 70% of girls say they have wanted to look like an actress. About 30% have actually tried to.

Young people can benefit from realizing how much they are being targeted as a consumer group and how media messages are used to either sell them products or convey messages about body image, self-esteem, social values, and behavior.

Source: www.riverdeep.net

D Complete each statement, according to the article. Then explain your answers.

1. The media can be damaging to a young person's ....
   a. self-image   **b.** high self-esteem   **c.** self-pity

2. If girls had more ...., they would not want to look like fashion models.
   a. self-pity   **b.** self-confidence   **c.** self-image

3. Before the age of ten, most girls are ....
   a. self-conscious   **b.** self-confident   **c.** self-critical

4. After the age of ten, a lot of teenage girls suffer from ....
   a. too much self-confidence   **b.** high self-esteem   **c.** low self-esteem

E Discussion.

1. Are girls and women in your country affected by images in the media? Are boys and men also affected? How?

2. What do you think young people can do to avoid being affected by the messages they get from advertising, TV, and the movies? What can they do to be more satisfied with the way they look and to develop their self-esteem?

DISCUSSION **BUILDER** • *Now describe what makes a person beautiful.*

Step 1. Pair Work. Take the survey. Then compare and explain your choices.

How much do you agree with each statement about men and women in your country?

	strongly disagree				strongly agree
1. Most women are self-conscious about their bodies.	1	2	3	4	5
2. Most men are self-conscious about their bodies.	1	2	3	4	5
3. Most women are self-conscious about their faces.	1	2	3	4	5
4. Most men are self-conscious about their faces.	1	2	3	4	5
5. Most women want to look more like people in the media.	1	2	3	4	5
6. Most men want to look more like people in the media.	1	2	3	4	5
7. Most women think beauty is not important.	1	2	3	4	5
8. Most men think beauty is not important.	1	2	3	4	5

Step 2. What do you think makes a person beautiful "on the outside"? How about "on the inside"? Take notes on your notepad.

Beauty on the outside	Beauty on the inside
a friendly face	a creative mind

Beauty on the outside	Beauty on the inside

Step 3. Discussion.

1. What is more important to you—a person's beauty on the outside or on the inside? Explain.

2. Do you think life is easier for people who are attractive? Why or why not?

3. Do you think people should just accept the way they look or try to change their appearances?

Writing: Compare two people's tastes in fashion

Compare and contrast

Connecting words can help a writer examine similarities and differences.

Compare (show similarities)	Contrast (show differences)
like Like Sylvia, I wear jeans all the time.	**but** Wendy wears fashionable clothes, **but** her sister does not.

similarly
I grew up paying little attention to fashion.
  Similarly, Mel was not very interested in clothes.
OR I grew up paying little attention to fashion;
  similarly, Mel was not very interested in clothes.
	however
	Lily had to wear a uniform when she was in school.
	  However, I was able to wear anything I wanted.
	OR Lily had to wear a uniform when she was in school;
	  however, I was able to wear anything I wanted.

too / also
Henry used to wear faded jeans in high school.
  I did **too**.
OR I did **also**.
OR I **also** did.
	whereas / while
	Sam spends a lot of money on clothes, **whereas**
	  Jeff shops in thrift stores.
	OR Sam spends a lot of money on clothes, **while**
	  Jeff shops in thrift stores.

Step 1. Prewriting. Organizing ideas.

Choose a topic. Then on a separate sheet of paper, draw a diagram similar to the one on the right. Label the circles with the topics you are comparing and write <u>Both</u> in the middle. List the differences in each circle and the similarities in the middle.

Step 2. Writing. On a separate sheet of paper, write two paragraphs comparing and contrasting ideas within the topic you chose, referring to the notes in your diagram. In your first paragraph, write about the differences. In your second paragraph, write about the similarities. Remember to use connecting words and include a topic sentence for each paragraph.

Step 3. Self-Check.

☐ Did you correctly use connecting words for comparing?

☐ Did you correctly use connecting words for contrasting?

☐ Does each paragraph have a topic sentence?

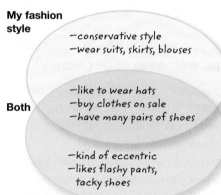

My fashion style
—conservative style
—wear suits, skirts, blouses

Both
—like to wear hats
—buy clothes on sale
—have many pairs of shoes

—kind of eccentric
—likes flashy pants, tacky shoes

My brother's fashion style

Topics
- Compare and contrast your fashion style with that of someone you know.
- Compare and contrast fashion today with fashion five, ten, or twenty years ago.

WRITING MODEL

  My brother Eric and I have very different tastes in fashion. I wear conservative clothes, **while** he prefers more eccentric outfits. He thinks he looks good in his flashy clothes, **but** I think his style is unattractive.

  However, there are some similarities in our styles. Eric likes to wear hats, and I do **too**. **Like** Eric, I am not

SUMMIT WEBSITE
For Unit 4 online activities, visit the *Summit* Companion Website at www.longman.com/summit.

A 🎧 **Listening Comprehension.** Listen carefully to the conversations about tastes in fashion. Infer which adjective best describes what each person thinks.

1. The man thinks the suit is ....
   a. stylish **b.** out of style **c.** tacky

2. The woman thinks the dress is ....
   a. chic **b.** old-fashioned **c.** flashy

3. The man thinks the tie is ....
   a. fashionable **b.** out of style **c.** shocking

4. The woman thinks the shoes are ....
   a. out of style **b.** in style **c.** striking

B Complete each statement with an appropriate word or phrase.

1. A set of rules for how to dress in a particular situation is a dress ....

2. In the United States and Canada, many companies allow their employees to wear "business ...." on Fridays—they don't have to wear suits, skirts, or ties.

3. Some companies allow employees to dress .... for some business meetings where the focus is on getting to know each other in a more casual setting.

4. When a fashion is .... style, people no longer wear that fashion. When a fashion is .... style, everyone wants to wear it.

C Cross out the one quantifier that *cannot* be used in each sentence.

1. (Every / A few / Most) older people find today's fashions pretty shocking.

2. Our company says that it will allow us to dress down (one / a couple of / a few) days a week.

3. (Most / Many / Every) young girls aren't worried about the way they look.

4. (Much / A majority of / A number of) researchers are concerned about the effect the media has on young boys as well.

5. (Many / Most / Much) men wore their hair very short in the 1930s.

6. I'd say your sister could use (some / a little / a few) fashion help.

7. There are (several / most / many) reasons why so many people have eating disorders.

8. A new study says that (most / many / every) children who watch TV for more than six hours a day may have problems with self-esteem as teenagers.

D **Writing.** Write a paragraph explaining your opinion about one of these expressions. Give concrete examples from your life.

"Beauty is only skin-deep." "Beauty is in the eye of the beholder."

Community

UNIT GOALS

1 Politely ask someone not to do something
2 Complain about public conduct
3 Discuss social responsibility
4 Identify urban problems

A **Topic Preview.** Look at the graph and photos. Where do most people live in your country—in rural or urban areas?

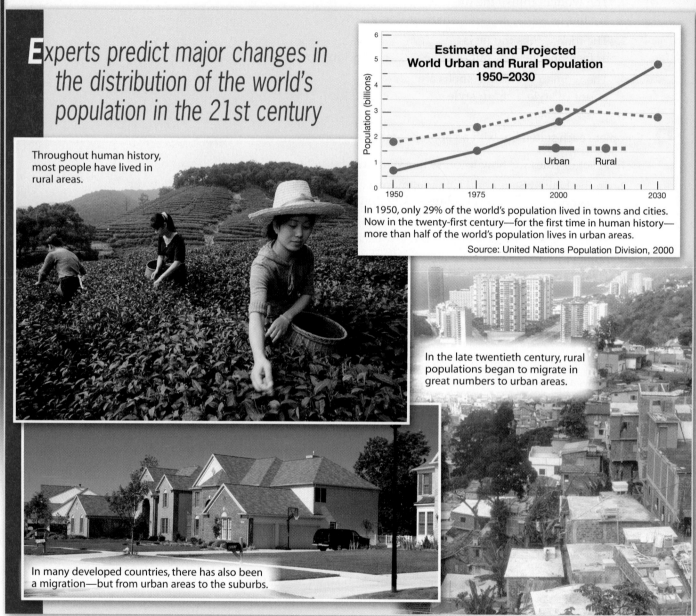

Experts predict major changes in the distribution of the world's population in the 21st century

Throughout human history, most people have lived in rural areas.

Estimated and Projected World Urban and Rural Population 1950–2030

Population (billions)

Urban   Rural

In 1950, only 29% of the world's population lived in towns and cities. Now in the twenty-first century—for the first time in human history—more than half of the world's population lives in urban areas.

Source: United Nations Population Division, 2000

In the late twentieth century, rural populations began to migrate in great numbers to urban areas.

In many developed countries, there has also been a migration—but from urban areas to the suburbs.

B **Pair Work.** Answer the questions, according to the information in the graph.

1. Approximately how many people in the world will be living in urban areas in 2030? How about in rural areas?

2. In what year did the world's urban population surpass the world's rural population?

C **Discussion.** Is there much migration in your country? What are some reasons people migrate?

PREVIEW

D 🎧 **Sound Bites.** Read and listen to a conversation about city life.

DON: Hey, Kyle! So how's the big city treating you?

KYLE: Funny you should ask. Not great.

DON: What do you mean?

KYLE: Well, on my way here, I'm crossing the street and this guy in an SUV turns the corner and almost runs me over.

DON: Are you serious?

KYLE: Yeah. The driver was in such a big hurry he didn't even notice. I just can't keep up with the pace here.

DON: Well, you *do* have to learn to stay on your toes in the city.

KYLE: It really gets to me sometimes. I don't think I'll ever get used to it. I guess I'm just a country boy at heart.

"the city"

E **In Other Words.** Read the conversation again. With a partner, explain the meaning of each of the following statements or questions.

1. "So how's the big city treating you?"

2. "I just can't keep up with the pace here."

3. "You *do* have to learn to stay on your toes."

4. "It really gets to me sometimes."

5. "I'm just a country boy at heart."

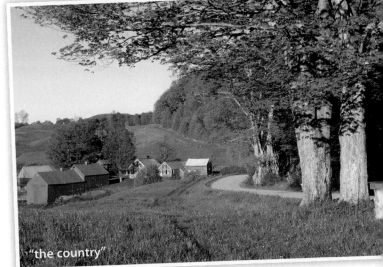

"the country"

STARTING **POINT**

What are some advantages and disadvantages of living in each type of place? Write them in the chart.

	Advantages	Disadvantages
the country		
the city		
the suburbs		

Discussion. Where would you prefer to live—in the country, the city, or the suburbs? Why?

Politely ask someone not to do something

A ⌒ CONVERSATION **SNAPSHOT**

A: Do you mind my smoking here?

B: Actually, smoking kind of bothers me.
I hope that's not a problem.

A: Not at all. I can step outside.

B: That's very considerate of you. Thanks
for asking.

⌒ **Rhythm and intonation practice**

> ⌒ **Ways to soften an objection**
>
> I hope that's not a problem.
> I hope you don't mind.
> I hope it's OK / all right.
> I don't mean to inconvenience you.

B Grammar. **Possessives with gerunds**

You can use a possessive before a gerund when you want to indicate the performer of the action.
The kids' singing was too loud.
Your constant **arguing** is getting on my nerves.
I didn't like **their talking** during the movie.
You should complain about **Sam's cutting** in line.
The thing that bothers me is **her smoking**.

In informal spoken English, a noun or an object pronoun is often used instead of a possessive.
I can understand **John being** annoyed. (instead of "John's being annoyed")
I can't accept **them ignoring** me. (instead of "their ignoring me")

C Combine the two statements, using a possessive with a gerund.

Example: They allow smoking. I'm not in favor of it.
      I'm not in favor of their allowing smoking.

1. He plays his MP3 player in the library. I don't appreciate that.

2. They smoke cigars in the car. My mother objects to it.

3. She's talking on her cell phone. We don't mind it.

4. My brother litters. I'm really annoyed by it.

D 🎧 **Word Skills.** Using negative prefixes to form antonyms

1. acceptable → **un**acceptable
2. considerate → **in**considerate
3. polite → **im**polite
4. proper → **im**proper
5. respectful → **dis**respectful
6. responsible → **ir**responsible

Negative prefixes

dis-	ir-
im-	un-
in-	

Pronunciation Booster

PAGE P4
Unstressed syllables

E **Pair Work.** Use a dictionary to find antonyms for the following words. What other adjectives can you find with negative prefixes?

1. appropriate → ....
2. courteous → ....
3. excusable → ....
4. imaginable → ....
5. honest → ....
6. pleasant → ....
7. rational → ....
8. mature → ....

F Write your own examples of inappropriate behavior. Use the adjectives from Exercises D and E.

Example: *It's inconsiderate to play loud music on a bus.*

1. ....
2. ....
3. ....
4. ....
5. ....

CONVERSATION **STARTER** • *Now politely ask someone not to do something.*

Pair Work. Discuss situations in which you would probably ask for permission to do something. Make a list on your notepad.

smoking in a restaurant
turning on the TV in a doctor's waiting room
making a call on my cell phone in public

Your list:

Role Play. Role-play a conversation in which you ask your partner for permission to do something. Your partner politely asks you not to do it. Use the Conversation Snapshot on page 52 as a guide. Start like this: "Do you mind my ..."

"Do you mind my smoking?"

"Do you mind my making a quick call on my cell phone?"

Complain about public conduct

GRAMMAR

A 🎧 GRAMMAR **SNAPSHOT.** Read the interview responses and notice the use of paired conjunctions.

What ticks you off?

**Wendy Kwon, 23
Chicago, USA**

What ticks me off? Well, I can't understand why people litter. Who do they think is going to clean up after them? **Either** they should throw their garbage in a trash can **or** hold on to it till they find one. I think it's great that people have to pay a fine for littering. Maybe they'll think twice before doing it again.

**Dana Fraser, 36
Toronto, Canada**

You know what gets to me? Smoking. It's such an inconsiderate habit. Secondhand cigarette smoke is **neither** good for you **nor** pleasant to be around. I'd like to see smoking banned from more public places. Don't non-smokers have rights too?

**Yuan Yong Jing, 28
Beijing, China**

It really bugs me when people spit on the street. **Not only** do I find it disgusting, **but** it's **also** unhygienic. It's important to think about other people's feelings and public health.

**Jorge Santos, 31
São Paulo, Brazil**

Here's something that gets on my nerves: I hate it when people use their cell phones in public places. They annoy other people, **not only** on trains and buses **but also** in theaters. They should have the courtesy to **either** turn their phones off **or** to leave them at home. It really makes me angry. I guess it's kind of my pet peeve.

B **Pair Work.** Do any of the behaviors described in the interview responses "tick you off"? With a partner, discuss and rate each of them as follows:

| extremely annoying | somewhat annoying | not annoying at all |

C **Grammar. Paired conjunctions**

You can connect related ideas with paired conjunctions.

either . . . or
   Either smoke outside **or** don't smoke at all.
   Cell phones should **either** be turned off **or** left at home.

neither . . . nor
   I would allow **neither** spitting **nor** littering on the street.
   Neither eating **nor** chewing gum is acceptable in class.

not only . . . but (also)
   Not only CD players **but also** cell phones should be banned from trains.

PAGE G9
For more ...

BE CAREFUL! When **not only . . . but (also)** joins two clauses, notice the subject–verb position in the first clause of the sentence.
   Not only **did they forget** to turn off their cell phones, but they also talked loudly during the concert.
   Not only **are they** noisy, but they're rude.

Verb agreement with paired conjunctions
When joining two subjects, make sure the verb agrees with the subject closer to the verb.
   Either the mayor or **local businesspeople need** to decide.
   Either local businesspeople or **the mayor needs** to decide.

D On a separate sheet of paper, combine the sentences with the paired conjunction indicated. Use or, nor, or but (also).

1. My uncle isn't willing to give up smoking. My grandparents aren't willing to give up smoking. (neither)

2. People should speak up about what bothers them. They should just learn to live with other people's habits. (either)

3. I don't like it when people use cell phones in theaters. I don't like it when they use them on buses. (not only)

4. The smell of the smoke bothers me. The danger to my health bothers me. (not only)

GRAMMAR **EXCHANGE** • *Now complain about public conduct.*

On your notepad, make a list of some of the things that really get on your nerves in public places. Then write sentences with paired conjunctions to express your opinion. Use some of the adjectives you already know.

IDEAS
- cutting in line
- graffiti on walls
- talking in theaters
- strong perfumes
- gossiping

In restaurants: *talking on cell phones*
It's not only annoying, but it's also very impolite.

In restaurants:

In stores:

On buses and trains:

On the street:

In offices:

In movie theaters:

Other:

Some adjectives
disrespectful
immature
impolite
inconsiderate
inexcusable
irresponsible
unacceptable
unpleasant

Group Work. One student is an "on-the-street interviewer" and asks the other students about what gets on their nerves. Use the sentences from your notepad in your responses.

What really ticks me off is ...

I'll tell you what really gets on my nerves. . . .

I can't understand why ...

You want to know what really bugs me?

Discussion.

1. In your opinion, how should people behave in public places? Do you think it's important to speak up when people behave inconsiderately in public?

2. Do *you* ever do things that annoy other people? Explain.

3 *Discuss social responsibility*

A 🎧 **Vocabulary.** **Ways to perform community service.** Listen and practice.

GET INVOLVED WITH YOUR COMMUNITY!

Beautify your town
Plant flowers or trees where there aren't any.

Clean up litter
Pick up trash from parks, playgrounds, or the street.

Donate your time
Mail letters, make phone calls, raise money, or collect signatures for a community service organization.

Volunteer
Work without pay in the fire department, a hospital, or a school.

Donate your organs
Save someone's life by making arrangements <u>now</u> to give your heart, lungs, and other organs after you die to someone who needs them.

B **Pair Work.** Would you ever consider doing any of the community service activities in the vocabulary? With a partner, explain why you would or would not.

> *"I would never consider donating my organs because it's against my beliefs."*

C 🎧 **Listening Comprehension.** Read the questions and listen to Part 1 of the story about Nicholas Green and his family. Take notes on your notepad. Then summarize the first part of the story with your partner.

Where were the Greens from?

What were they doing in Italy?

What happened to Nicholas?

What decision did his parents make?

How did the Italian people react?

Nicholas Green, age seven, in Switzerland, a few days before he and his family went to Italy

D 🎧 Read the questions and listen to Part 2. Discuss your answers with a partner.

1. What changes occurred in Italy after the Greens made their decision? What is "The Nicholas Effect"?

2. How many people received one of Nicholas's organs? What effect did his gift have on their lives?

3. As a result of this incident, what are the Greens doing today?

E **Discussion.**

1. Do you think you would have made the same decision the Greens did if you had been in their situation? Why or why not?

2. Why do you think people responded so strongly to this story?

DISCUSSION **BUILDER** • *Now discuss social responsibility.*

Step 1. Pair Work. Consider each situation and discuss what you might do. Based on your answers, how strong do you think your "sense of community" is?

"My first responsibility is to my family. I can't imagine doing this for a total stranger."

"I'd be happy to donate money to help a stranger. People should help each other."

1 There has been a terrible storm, and many homes have been destroyed. You're asked to let a family live with you until their home is fixed.

What would you do if they were . . .

   a. your relatives?   c. your colleague's family?

   b. your neighbors?   d. complete strangers?

2 Someone needs a new liver to survive. Doctors say that they can use a piece of your liver to save that person's life.

What would you do if the person were . . .

   a. a family member?   c. your classmate?

   b. your neighbor?   d. a complete stranger?

3 Developers plan to destroy a well-known historical monument so they can build a new office building. You're asked to donate your time to help save that monument.

What would you do if the monument were . . .

   a. in your neighborhood?   c. in another city in your country?

   b. in another part of the city? d. in another country?

Step 2. Discussion. Have you or someone you know ever volunteered for some kind of community service? How important is it for a person to be active in his or her community? Explain.

4 Identify urban problems

A **Reading Warm-up.** What problems do you think cities of 10 million or more people might share?

B 🎧 **Reading.** Read the interview. Do you agree with Dr. Perlman's views?

The Advent of the Megacity

Following is an interview with Dr. Janice Perlman, founder and president of Mega-Cities Project, Inc. Her organization attempts to make cities worldwide more livable places by taking good ideas from one place and trying to make them work in another.

Q. How do you define "megacity"?

A. We define megacities in our work as cities that have reached populations of 10 million or more. The majority of these are in developing countries. Migration to the city is the route for many people to greater choice, opportunity, and well-being. By coming to settle in the city, they have in effect "voted with their feet."

Q. Why are these places going to be very important in the next hundred years?

A. The 21st century won't be a century of rural areas and small towns but of giant cities that will set the standard of how we live, how our environment is preserved (or not preserved), how our economies work, and what kind of civil society we develop.

Mexico City over 18 million (2005)

Tokyo over 28 million (2005)

Q. Do megacities in the developed and developing world differ, or are they linked by certain similarities?

A. These large cities have a lot more in common with each other than they do with the small towns and villages in their own countries. For example, every megacity struggles with a widening gap between rich and poor. Every "first-world" city, such as Los Angeles, New York, London, or Tokyo, has within it a "third-world" city of poverty and deprivation. And every third-world city, such as Calcutta, Cairo, or Mexico City, has within it a first-world city of high culture, technology, fashion, and finance.

In addition, all megacities share the problems of providing jobs and economic opportunities, and making housing, education, and health care available. They deal with crime and violence, as well as basic infrastructure such as water, sanitation, and public transportation. This is no easy task. The leaders of these cities recognize that they have similar problems, and they would like to learn more from other cities, particularly about successful solutions.

If we are going to create livable cities for the next century, we will need to be clever enough to do it through collaboration and cooperation. That is why the Mega-Cities Project works to share experiences that work across boundaries of culture and geography.

Q. Is the solution to urban problems strict central planning?

A. Absolutely not. We need decentralized planning that includes local citizens. In my view, attempts to create planned cities or communities—like Brasília or Chandigarh—are too sterile and miss the spontaneity of cities that grew organically, like Rio de Janeiro, Bombay, or even New York City. The best example of urban planning I've seen recently is in Curitiba, Brazil, which set up a brilliant public transportation system in anticipation of population growth. The historic areas of cities like Siena, Paris, or Barcelona all have elements of planning that led to buildings of similar heights and architecture, but they were not centrally planned. There is a lot of diversity within the design, and people love to go to those cities.

Megacities are really very exciting places. The truth is, I've never met a megacity that I didn't like!

The World's Ten Largest Urban Areas	Population (millions) in 1996	in 2015	Rank in 2015
1 Tokyo, Japan	27.2	28.9	1
2 Mexico City, Mexico	16.9	19.2	7
3 São Paulo, Brazil	16.8	20.3	4
4 New York, United States	16.4	17.6	9
5 Mumbai (Bombay), India	15.7	26.2	2
6 Shanghai, China	13.7	18	8
7 Los Angeles, United States	12.6	14.2	15
8 Kolkata (Calcutta), India	12.1	17.3	10
9 Buenos Aires, Argentina	11.9	13.9	17
10 Seoul, Korea	11.8	13	19

Source: U.N. Department of Economic and Social Affairs Population Division

Source: http://usinfo.state.gov

C Check the types of urban problems Dr. Perlman mentions or suggests in the interview.

☐ poverty   ☐ pollution   ☐ unemployment   ☐ inadequate public
☐ lack of housing ☐ disease   ☐ discrimination   transportation
☐ crowding   ☐ crime   ☐ corruption

D **Understanding Meaning from Context.** Read each statement from the interview.
Then choose the sentence that is closest to what Dr. Perlman means. Use information from the
reading to help explain your answers.

1. "By coming to settle in the city, they have in effect 'voted with their feet.'"
   a. People are making it clear which kind of life they prefer.
   b. People would rather live in the country than live in the city.
   c. People don't have as much opportunity in the city as they do in the country.

2. "Every 'first-world' city . . . has within it a 'third-world' city of poverty and
   deprivation. And every third-world city . . . has within it a first-world city of high
   culture, technology, fashion, and finance."
   a. Some megacities have more poverty than others.
   b. All megacities have both poverty and wealth.
   c. Some megacities have more wealth than others.

3. "The Mega-Cities Project works to share experiences that work across boundaries of
   culture and geography."
   a. The Mega-Cities Project helps megacities communicate their success stories to the
      people who live in that city.
   b. The Mega-Cities Project helps megacities communicate their success stories to
      other cities in that country.
   c. The Mega-Cities Project helps megacities communicate their success stories to
      megacities in other countries.

E **Discussion.**

1. Why does Dr. Perlman say she prefers cities that are *not* planned over planned cities?

2. Why do you think Dr. Perlman thinks megacities are exciting? Do you agree?

3. Do you live in a megacity, or have you ever visited one? What are the pros and cons
   of living in a megacity?

4. Do you think life in megacities will improve in the future or get worse? Why?

DISCUSSION **BUILDER** • *Now identify urban problems.*

Step 1. Pair Work. Check which urban problems
you think exist in your area. Discuss and provide
examples.

Step 2. Discussion. Talk about the problems you've
identified. As a group, discuss at least five ways
to make improvements in your town or city.

○ poverty   ○ pollution
○ crime   ○ corruption
○ crowding   ○ lack of housing
○ disease   ○ discrimination
○ inadequate public   ○ unemployment
  transportation   ○ other: _____

Step 3. Writing. Describe the social problems that exist in your town or city.
Suggest some possible solutions.

Writing: Complain about a problem

Formal letters

When writing to a friend or family member, an informal tone, casual language, and abbreviations are acceptable. However, when writing to the head of a company, a boss, or someone you don't know, standard formal language should be used, and regular spelling and punctuation rules apply. Formal letters are usually typewritten, not handwritten. The following salutations and closings are appropriate for formal letters:

Formal salutations	Formal closings
Dear [Mr. / Mrs. / Ms. / Dr. / Professor Smyth]:	Sincerely,
Dear Sir or Madam:	Respectfully (yours),
To whom it may concern:	Cordially,

When writing a formal letter of complaint, first state the reason why you are writing and the problem. Then inform whomever you are writing what you would like him or her to do about it, or what *you* plan to do.

WRITING MODEL

4719 McPherson Avenue
Philadelphia, Pennsylvania 19102
June 30, 2006

Red Maple Café
708 West Pine Street
Philadelphia, Pennsylvania 19102

Salutation —[Dear Sir or Madam:

    I live a few blocks from your restaurant. For the past several months, I have noticed that in the evenings there is a lot of trash on the side of your building. Cats in the neighborhood turn over the garbage cans, and the trash goes everywhere. This is not only unpleasant to look at, but it is also a health hazard.

    Could you please make sure that when the trash is put out, the garbage cans are closed? Your helping keep our neighborhood clean and beautiful would be greatly appreciated.

Closing —[Respectfully,

Olivia Krum

Olivia Krum

Step 1. Prewriting. Listing ideas. Think of a problem in your community that you would like to complain about. List the reasons why it is a problem.

> Problem: *trash on side of building*
> Reasons: *—unpleasant to look at*
>   *—health hazard*

Problem:

Reasons:

Step 2. Writing. On a separate sheet of paper, use your notes to write a letter of complaint. State what you intend to do or what you would like to see done. Remember to use the appropriate level of formality.

Step 3. Self-Check.

☐ Did you use the proper salutation and closing?

☐ Are the tone and language in the letter appropriate for the audience?

☐ Did you use regular spelling and punctuation and avoid abbreviations?

Step 4. Peer Response. Exchange letters with a partner. Write an appropriate response to your partner's letter, as if you were the person to whom it was addressed.

SUMMIT WEBSITE
For Unit 5 online activities, visit the *Summit* Companion Website at www.longman.com/summit.

A 🎧 **Listening Comprehension.** Listen carefully to the conversations about cities. Check the adjectives that are closest in meaning to what the people say about each place. Listen again if necessary.

	rich	poor	clean	polluted	safe	dangerous	polite people	rude people	interesting	boring
1. rural China	○	○	○	○	○	○	○	○	○	○
2. Los Angeles	○	○	○	○	○	○	○	○	○	○
3. Singapore	○	○	○	○	○	○	○	○	○	○
4. Paris	○	○	○	○	○	○	○	○	○	○

B Respond to each question in your *own* way.

1. "Do you mind if I call someone on my cell phone?"

YOU ....

2. "Would you mind not smoking in here?"

YOU ....

3. "What bugs you about living in your town?"

YOU ....

4. "Who do you know that really gets on your nerves?"

YOU ....

C Make each sentence logical by attaching a negative prefix to one of the adjectives. Use a dictionary if necessary.

1. Painting graffiti on public buses and trains is really excusable.

2. I believe littering and spitting on the street are responsible behaviors.

3. Young people who play loud music without consideration for the people around them are exhibiting really proper behavior.

4. I think it's very appropriate for people to scream into their cell phones in theaters.

5. When a salesperson is rude, I find it not only respectful but also annoying.

6. I should warn you that the air pollution downtown is really pleasant.

7. I think politicians who are honest and corrupt should be punished.

8. It doesn't help when people are courteous to each other.

D Combine the sentences with the paired conjunction indicated. Use <u>or</u>, <u>nor</u>, or <u>but (also)</u>.

1. Restaurants shouldn't allow smoking. Theaters shouldn't allow smoking. (neither)

....

2. Smoking should be banned. It should be restricted. (either)

....

3. Littering doesn't offend me. Spitting doesn't offend me. (neither)

....

4. I think loud music is rude. I think loud people are rude. (not only)

....

UNIT 6

Animals

UNIT GOALS

1 Exchange opinions about the treatmer of animals
2 Discuss the benefits of certain pets
3 Compare animal characters
4 Debate the value of animal conservatic

A **Topic Preview.** Find your birth year on the Chinese Zodiac. What's your animal sign?

TIGER

1938 1950 1962
1974 1986 1998
Self-confident, independent, and emotional. Sometimes you tend to be inconsiderate and selfish.

RABBIT

1939 1951 1963
1975 1987 1999
Intelligent, kind, and helpful. You are also traditional and somewhat conservative. You tend to tell people what's on your mind.

OX

1937 1949 1961
1973 1985 1997
Hardworking, serious, and responsible. You can sometimes be a workaholic. It's difficult to get you to change your opinions and beliefs, and you get angry easily.

DRAGON

1940 1952 1964
1976 1988 2000
Fun loving, artistic, and truthful. You don't always feel confident in yourself or your abilities. You are also a little eccentric at times.

RAT

1936 1948 1960
1972 1984 1996
Generous, honest, and imaginative. You are usually careful, and sometimes you are a perfectionist.

SNAKE

1941 1953 1965
1977 1989 2001
Attractive and very calm. You are able to make good decisions and give good advice. Sometimes you can be self-centered.

BOAR

1947 1959 1971
1983 1995 2007
Generally quiet and honest. You work hard toward your goals. You don't have many friends, but you are very considerate to the friends you have.

HORSE

1942 1954 1966
1978 1990 2002
Popular, outgoing, and cheerful. You are a real people person. Sometimes you are too talkative.

DOG

1946 1958 1970
1982 1994 2006
Honest, caring, and modest. You are always there for your friends. You may at times seem cold and unfriendly to people who don't know you.

GOAT

1943 1955 1967
1979 1991 2003
Passionate, very artistic, and a bit shy. You are good at understanding other people's problems. Sometimes you are too willing to believe what other people say.

MONKEY

1944 1956 1968
1980 1992 2004
Clever and likable. You have new and interesting ideas, and you learn very quickly. Sometimes you can also be a little egotistical.

ROOSTER

1945 1957 1969
1981 1993 2005
Attractive and self-confident. You want to be very successful. Sometimes you say things just to make people look up to you.

Source: silverdragonstudio.com

B **Discussion.**

1. How well do the adjectives for your sign describe your personality? How are you different from the description?

2. Do you think the descriptions match the animals in any way? Why or why not?

C 🎧 **Sound Bites.** Read and listen to a conversation between two friends at the zoo.

ALICIA: I can't believe I let you talk me into coming here. I really have a problem with zoos.

BEN: C'mon. These guys have got it made. They're well-cared for. They're healthy. They've got plenty of food.

ALICIA: You could say the same thing about people in prisons. What about freedom? I hate seeing animals cooped up in cages.

BEN: You think animals are any happier in the wild? Always hungry? Running from some bigger animal that's trying to eat them?

ALICIA: I don't know. Maybe not.

BEN: Just look at that tiger over there. Where else could you see such a beautiful animal up close?

ALICIA: You're right about that. He *is* magnificent.

Giraffes in the zoo

D **Pair Work.** Read the conversation again. Discuss the questions and explain your answers.

1. What is Alicia's objection to zoos?

2. How is Ben's attitude different from Alicia's?

3. What does Ben mean when he says, "These guys have got it made"?

4. What do Alicia and Ben agree on about zoos?

STARTING **POINT**

Pair Work. What adjectives do you associate with different animals? Choose five adjectives and discuss with a partner an animal you think each adjective describes.

frightening

unusual

fun

friendly

calm

irritating

attractive

loving

unfriendly

independent

shy

disgusting

hardworking

quiet

ADJECTIVE	ANIMAL
1.	
2.	
3.	
4.	
5.	

Exchange opinions about the treatment of animals

A 🎧 GRAMMAR **SNAPSHOT.** Read the posts on a discussion board and notice the use of passive modals.

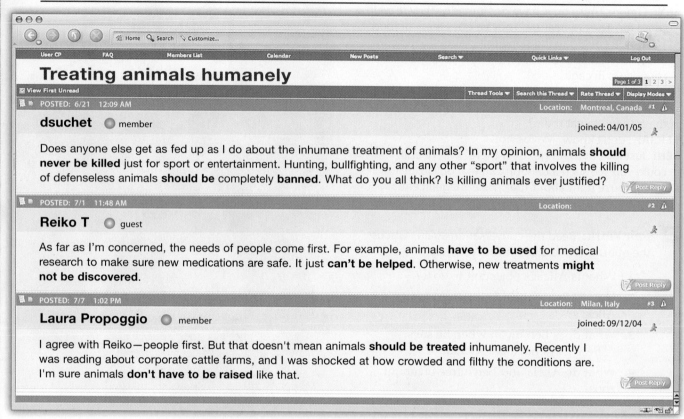

Treating animals humanely

POSTED: 6/21   12:09 AM   Location: Montreal, Canada #1

dsuchet ● member   joined: 04/01/05

Does anyone else get as fed up as I do about the inhumane treatment of animals? In my opinion, animals **should never be killed** just for sport or entertainment. Hunting, bullfighting, and any other "sport" that involves the killing of defenseless animals **should be** completely **banned**. What do you all think? Is killing animals ever justified?

POSTED: 7/1   11:48 AM   Location: #2

Reiko T ● guest

As far as I'm concerned, the needs of people come first. For example, animals **have to be used** for medical research to make sure new medications are safe. It just **can't be helped**. Otherwise, new treatments **might not be discovered**.

POSTED: 7/7   1:02 PM   Location: Milan, Italy   #3

Laura Propoggio ● member   joined: 09/12/04

I agree with Reiko—people first. But that doesn't mean animals **should be treated** inhumanely. Recently I was reading about corporate cattle farms, and I was shocked at how crowded and filthy the conditions are. I'm sure animals **don't have to be raised** like that.

B **Discussion.** Do you agree with any of the opinions expressed on the discussion board? Why or why not?

C Grammar. **The passive voice with modals**

Can for present possibility or ability
Alternatives **can be found** for medical research on animals.

Might (not) and could for present or future possibility
New medicines **might be discovered** through animal testing.
Cattle **might not be mistreated** if people knew about the conditions.
A lot **could be done** to improve conditions.

Couldn't and can't for present impossibility
Research **couldn't be done** today without animals.
Sometimes testing on animals **can't be helped**.

Should and shouldn't for advisability
Corporate chicken farms **should be shut down**.
People **shouldn't be prohibited** from hunting.

Have to and must for necessity
Some animals **have to be killed**.
Traditions like bullfighting **must be preserved**.
NOTE: **Must** is rarely used in informal English.

Yes / no questions
Can other types of research **be found**?
Should factory farms **be shut down**?
Must animals **be used** for research?
Do animals **have to be used** for research?

Information questions
How **can** animals **be trained** to help humans?
What **could be done** to improve conditions?
Why **must** their lives **be respected**?
Why **do** their lives **have to be respected**?

BE CAREFUL! **Don't have to / doesn't have to** expresses a lack of necessity, but **must not** expresses prohibition.
Animals **don't have to be killed** for research.
[= it is not necessary]
Animals **must not be killed** for research.
[= it should be prohibited]

Grammar Booster

PAGE G10
For more …

D Write sentences using modals and the correct form of the passive voice.

1. People / should / allow to hunt deer. ....

2. Alternatives to animal research / might / discover. ....

3. Wild animals / shouldn't / keep as pets. ....

4. Fox hunting / should / ban. ....

5. The treatment of animals / could / improve. ....

E 🎧 **Vocabulary. Ways animals are used or treated.** Listen and practice.

They're **kept in zoos.**

They're **used for medical research.**

They're **killed for their hides and fur.**

They're **trained to perform in circuses.**

They're **raised for fighting.**

They're **trained to help people with disabilities.**

They're **slaughtered for food.**

They're **used for racing.**

F On a separate sheet of paper, write your opinion about each of the ways animals are used or treated. Use the passive voice with modals.

Animals should be kept in zoos so people can enjoy them.

GRAMMAR **EXCHANGE** • *Now exchange opinions about the treatment of animals.*

Pair Work. Exchange opinions about the ways animals are used or treated. Ask and answer questions, using passive modals.

*"Animals **have to be used** for medical research. We can't experiment on humans, can we?"*

*"Actually, I don't think animals **should be treated** that way. I think it's morally wrong."*

Expressing an opinion
I think / believe / feel . . .
    it's morally wrong.
    it's OK under some
        circumstances.
    it's wrong no matter what.
I'm in favor of ....
I'm opposed to ....

Disagreeing
I see what you mean, but ....
That's one way to look at it,
    but ....
On the one hand ...., but on
    the other hand ....
I completely disagree.

Agreeing
I couldn't agree with you more.
I completely agree.
You're so right.

Discussion. Compare your classmates' opinions on the treatment of animals. Does the majority of the class feel the same way?

Discuss the benefits of certain pets

A 🎧 CONVERSATION **SNAPSHOT**

A: I've been considering getting an iguana for a pet.

B: Are you out of your mind? I've heard they're filthy.

A: Actually, that's a misconception. Iguanas are very clean and make great pets.

B: In what way?

A: Well, for one thing, they're very intelligent. And believe it or not, I find them beautiful.

🎧 **Rhythm and intonation practice**

B 🎧 Vocabulary. Describing pets. Listen and practice.

Positive traits	
adorable	cute and charming
affectionate	exceptionally friendly and loving
gentle / good-natured	easygoing; good with people and other pets
low maintenance	easy to care for and inexpensive to keep
loyal / devoted	attentive to its owner; reliable

Negative traits	
aggressive	violent; sometimes dangerous
costly	expensive to buy and to take care of
destructive	harmful to furniture and other things
filthy	unclean; makes a mess
high maintenance	time-consuming to take care of

C 🎧 Listening Comprehension. Listen to the conversations about pets. Then listen again and complete the chart. Use adjectives you know that best describe the advantages and disadvantages the people talk about. Discuss if you think the people will get the pet.

	Pet	Advantages	Disadvantages
Conversation 1			
Conversation 2			
Conversation 3			
Conversation 4			

D **Discussion.**

1. Do you think that an animal can be a good companion? Why or why not?
2. Do you know anyone who is very attached to his or her pet? Why do you think some people get so close to their animals?

Pronunciation Booster

PAGE P5
Sound reduction

CONVERSATION **STARTER** • *Now discuss the benefits of certain pets.*

Pair Work. Which animals do you think make good pets or bad pets? Discuss and make a list on your notepad. Use the pictures or other animals you know. Write complete sentences, using the vocabulary.

Good pets	Why?
Bad pets	Why?

a parrot

Role Play. Role-play a conversation about getting a pet. Use the Conversation Snapshot on page 66 as a guide. Start like this: "I've been considering getting .... for a pet."

a pit bull

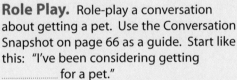

a pug

a Siamese cat

a python

a mouse

67

3 Compare animal characters

A 🎧 **Vocabulary.** **Describing character traits.** Listen and practice.

> **clever** able to use one's intelligence to do something
> **gullible** too ready to believe what other people say, and therefore easy to trick
> **mean** willing to hurt others, especially with words
> **selfish** caring only about oneself and not likely to share with others
> **sincere** saying what one really feels or believes
> **vain** too proud of one's looks, abilities, or position
> **wise** able to make good decisions and give good advice based on life experiences

B Complete each sentence with an adjective from the vocabulary.

1. Don't be so .... When something sounds too good to be true, it usually is!

2. He is so .... that he won't go out if his hair is a bit messy.

3. Carla is really open and .... You can always trust her to say what she means.

4. My parrot is so .... that he's learned how to say three new words this week.

5. Our neighbor is really .... When kids play in front of her house, she always yells at them.

6. My grandfather knew how to help me with my problems. He was really ....

7. It's normal for young children to be .... They usually don't want other children to play with their toys.

"The fox saw a crow in a tree."

C 🎧 **Listening Comprehension.** Listen to the fable of "The Fox and the Crow." Choose adjectives to describe each animal. Then listen again and write the moral, or the lesson, of the story in your *own* words.

> Adjectives for the fox
> ....
> Adjectives for the crow
> ....
> The moral of the story
> ....
> ....
> ....
> ....
> ....

D 🎧 Now listen to the fable of "The Peacock's Tail." Choose adjectives to describe each animal. Then listen again and write the moral of the story in your *own* words.

Adjectives for the peacock
....

Adjectives for the sparrow
....

The moral of the story
....

....

....

....

....

"*A small brown sparrow sat in a tree watching the peacock.*"

E **Discussion.**

1. How are the crow and the peacock alike? What trait or traits do they share?

2. Have you ever known anyone who has the same traits as the peacock, the crow, the fox, or the sparrow? Explain.

DISCUSSION **BUILDER** • *Now compare animal characters.*

Step 1. What are your favorite animal stories from books, cartoons, TV programs, or movies? Choose three animal characters and describe the animals' character traits on your notepad.

Animal characters	Character traits
1.	
2.	
3.	

Step 2. Pair Work. Compare and discuss the animal characters you chose. What moral or lesson about life do you think the characters try to teach?

Step 3. Discussion. Why do you think writers often use animals instead of people in stories? Why do you think so many children's stories are about animals?

4 Debate the value of animal conservation

A **Reading Warm-up.** What are some endangered animals you can think of? What are some threats to their survival?

B 🎧 **Reading.** Read the article. Do you agree with the point of view expressed?

Protecting Our Natural Inheritance

The polar bear's habitat is at risk.

The earth is rich in biodiversity with millions of different species of plants and animals. However, many species are disappearing at an alarming rate. Biodiversity is reduced when ecosystems are modified and habitats of plants and animals are destroyed. The one species that is causing this phenomenon is the same one that can stop it—humans.

Many scientists view the current wave of species extinctions as unrivaled since the disappearance of the dinosaurs, more than 65 million years ago. Currently, around 11,000 species of plants and animals are at risk of disappearing forever—this includes over 180 mammals.

There are only about 700 mountain gorillas left in the wild.

Many species cling to survival. Found only in China, the giant panda's habitat has been decimated—the old-growth bamboo forests where the pandas make their home are being destroyed rapidly. It is estimated that as few as 1,600 giant pandas remain in the wild today. In the Arctic, the polar bear's icy habitat is disappearing as a result of global warming, and its survival is at risk. And in Central and East Africa, which have endured decades of civil war, the mountain gorilla population now totals just over 700 individuals.

If present trends continue, humanity stands to lose a large portion of its natural inheritance. Extinction is one environmental problem that is truly irreversible—once gone, these species cannot be brought back.

What can be done? World Wildlife Fund (WWF), the global conservation organization,

China's giant panda clings to survival.

has been working since 1961 to conserve the diversity of life on earth. In recent years, WWF has advanced giant panda conservation by training more than 300 panda reserve staff and local government officials, working with the community to help save habitat and guard against illegal hunting. By spreading awareness of the danger of carbon dioxide emissions, and by promoting the use of renewable energy resources such as wind and solar power, WWF is trying to head off the effects of global warming, giving the polar bear a chance to survive. With the help of other organizations in Africa, WWF has established a system to monitor the status of mountain gorillas in order to be able to address potential threats.

Why care about endangered animals? There are many reasons for protecting endangered species, including our own survival. Many of our foods and medicines come from wild species, and each wild species depends on a particular habitat for its food and shelter, and ultimately its survival. If one species in an ecosystem disappears, other species are affected. And when one ecosystem is altered or destroyed, a ripple effect occurs, and the interdependency of all living things becomes clear. Animals not only need protection to ensure their own species' survival, but they also serve as umbrella species; helping them helps numerous other species that live in the same habitat.

Beyond economics and human well-being, however, the rapid extinction of so many creatures on our planet raises profound ethical and moral questions. What sort of world will our children inherit? Do we want the future to be a place where pandas and gorillas only exist in captivity in zoos? If we are unable—or unwilling—to protect the animals we share our planet with, what does that say about humankind's future on earth?

For more information on WWF and its work, visit www.worldwildlife.org.

70 UNIT 6

C **Understanding Meaning from Context.** Use the context of the article to determine the meaning of the words and phrases.

1. **biodiversity** (line 1)
   a. endangered animals   **b.** the variety of living things   **c.** threats to nature

2. **habitat** (lines 4, 24, 28, and 61)
   a. the food animals eat   **b.** the place animals live   **c.** the extinction of animals

3. **extinction** (lines 12, 36, and 72)
   a. global warming   **b.** trying to protect animals   **c.** the disappearance of a species

4. **conservation** (lines 40 and 45)
   a. trying to protect animals   **b.** dangers to animals   **c.** feeding animals

5. **ecosystem** (lines 4, 63, and 64)
   a. trying to protect animals   **b.** threats to animals   **c.** how plants and animals work together

D **Discussion.**

1. According to the article, what are some reasons animals become extinct? Can you think of any other reasons?

2. What arguments are given in the article to support animal conservation?

3. Look again at the last paragraph in the article. How would *you* answer the questions it raises?

DISCUSSION **BUILDER** • *Now debate the value of animal conservation.*

Step 1. Pair Work. Read and discuss the arguments for and against animal conservation. Which arguments are the strongest for each side of the animal conservation debate? Which are the weakest?

Pros	Cons
• Human beings have a responsibility to protect all living things.	• Extinctions are simply part of the natural process—it's the principle of "survival of the fittest."
• Species should be preserved for future generations.	• Environmental protection costs a lot of money. It's "a luxury" for countries that have more serious problems.
• Natural parks and wildlife are big tourist attractions—they generate jobs and income for local economies.	• Millions of species have already become extinct with no significant impact on the environment—it's no big deal.
• Species extinction at the current rate could lead to an ecological disaster.	• Conservation limits land available to farmers, who really need it for their livelihood.
• We miss the chance for new discoveries, such as medicines, with every species we lose.	• Do we really need 2,000 species of mice?
• Your own ideas:	• Your own ideas: ....

Step 2. Debate. Is it important to spend money on animal conservation? Form two groups—one for and one against. Take turns presenting your views.

Step 3. Discussion.

1. Why do you think some animals become endangered? What are some threats to the survival of animals in the wild?

2. In your opinion, are species worth saving even if they aren't "popular" or of any known value to people? Why or why not?

Writing: Express an opinion on animal treatment

Persuasion

To persuade readers to agree with your point of view, provide examples, facts, or experts' opinions that support your argument. Another effective technique is to demonstrate the weakness of opposing arguments. Summarize your main point in your concluding sentence.

Support your point of view	Offer experts' opinions
For example, . . .	[Smith] states that . . .
Another example is . . .	According to [Rivera], . . .
For instance, . . .	

Ways to discuss opposing arguments	Ways to conclude your argument
It can be argued that . . .	In conclusion, . . .
Some people think . . . } However,	In summary, . . .
It is true that . . .	To sum up, . . .

WRITING MODEL

Zoos play an important role in animal conservation. **For instance,** studies suggest that research is more easily conducted in zoos. **It can be argued that** animals should be free and that it is unethical to keep them in zoos. **However,** the survival of these species depends on scientific studies. **In conclusion,** animals should be kept in zoos in order to support conservation efforts.

Step 1. Prewriting. Planning your argument. Choose one of the questions in the following box or write your own question. State your opinion and list your arguments. Then think of possible opposing arguments.

- Is research on animals necessary in order to develop new medicines and procedures?
- Are some traditional forms of entertainment, such as circuses, bullfights, and cockfights, cruel to animals?
- Your own question: ....
  ....

Your opinion: ....

Your arguments:

1. ....
2. ....
3. ....

Possible opposing arguments:

1. ....
2. ....
3. ....

Step 2. Writing. On a separate sheet of paper, write a paragraph arguing your opinion from Step 1. Remember to include a topic sentence at the beginning of the paragraph and a concluding sentence at the end.

Step 3. Self-Check.

☐ Did you state your point of view clearly?

☐ Did you provide examples, facts, or experts' opinions to support your point of view?

☐ Did you discuss opposing arguments?

☐ Did you include a topic sentence and a concluding sentence?

Step 4. Peer Response. Exchange paragraphs with a partner. Do you agree or disagree with your partner's point of view? Write a short response, explaining why. Start like this: I agree / disagree because . . . .

WRITING

UNIT 6 CHECKPOINT

SUMMIT WEBSITE
For Unit 6 online activities, visit the
Summit Companion Website at
www.longman.com/summit.

A 🎧 **Listening Comprehension.** Listen to Part 1 of a radio program. Choose the phrase that best completes the statements, according to the listening.

1. Capuchin monkeys can be ....
   a. used for medical research   **b.** loyal friends to humans   **c.** trained to perform in circuses

2. These monkeys are useful to humans because they ....
   a. do simple jobs   **b.** push a wheelchair   **c.** wash dishes

B 🎧 Now listen to Part 2 and choose the phrase that best completes the statements.

1. Dolphin-assisted therapy had a positive effect on children's ....
   a. moral or ethical development   **b.** speech development   **c.** physical development

2. Children respond to dolphins because dolphins are ....
   a. good swimmers   **b.** intelligent   **c.** playful

3. Many of these children respond better to people after ....
   a. a year of treatment   **b.** a few treatments   **c.** a few weeks of treatment

C Change the adjective in each statement so it makes sense.

1. A relaxed pet that never bites is *destructive*. ....
2. A cat that bites or scratches people is *affectionate*. ....
3. A pet that likes to be with people is *aggressive*. ....
4. A dog that chews on shoes is *adorable*. ....
5. A pet that makes a mess is *sociable*. ....

D Complete each statement with an appropriate character trait.

1. A person who says or does unkind things to others is ....
2. People who can't pass a mirror without looking at themselves are ....
3. If one expresses oneself honestly to others, we say that person is ....
4. Someone who is too trusting of others is ....
5. People who think mainly about themselves are ....
6. People who are skillful at getting what they want are ....
7. If people have good judgment on matters of importance, we say they are ....

E Choose four of the topics from the box. Use modals with the passive voice to state your *own* opinion about each topic.

endangered animals	hunting	pets
horseracing	bullfighting	zoos

Example: *Hunting should be banned because it's inhumane.*

1. ....
2. ....
3. ....
4. ....

UNIT 7

Advertising and Consumers

UNIT GOALS

1 Give shopping advice
2 Discuss your reactions to ads
3 Persuade someone to buy a product
4 Describe consumer shopping habits

A **Topic Preview.** Look at the types of advertisements companies use to try to get consumers to buy products. What types of ads do you think you are most exposed to daily?

TV commercials

A BIKE THAT'S EASY TO CARE FOR. AND A BELT TO MATCH.

color perfectamente hermoso

magazine ads

ads on trains, buses, or blimps

AQUAFINA GET SPOTTED

Internet pop-ups

billboards

ContestAlley.com
Platinum Plus $7500

Be the first to own one!

我的网 MyWeb 我的网

www.myweb.com.cn

radio ads

B **Discussion.**

1. Which type of advertising do you find the most effective? Why?

2. Read the information to the right. Are you surprised by these statistics? Do you think they are similar for your country?

Daily Exposure to Advertising
In the United States, the average person is exposed to approximately 254 advertising messages each day—108 from TV, 34 from radio, and 112 from print. If you include brand labels on products and corporate logos on the sides of buildings, this number increases to over 1,000 ads per day.

Advertising Media Inter Center

C 🎧 **Sound Bites.** Read and listen to a couple talking about ads in a catalog.

BOB: I think it's about time I got myself one of these electric massage chairs.
ANN: What on earth for?
BOB: It would just be nice to have one. That's all.
ANN: Sounds like a waste of money to me. Don't they have anything useful in there?
BOB: See for yourself.
ANN: Now here's something I'd like to get my hands on—a self-watering flowerpot.
BOB: You've got to be kidding.
ANN: No, I'm not. I think one of these could come in really handy.

D **In Other Words.** Read the conversation again. With a partner, find an expression in the conversation that is similar in meaning to each of the following statements or questions.

1. Why would you do that?
2. That's a useless thing to buy.
3. I'd really love to have one.
4. You can't be serious.
5. It might be very useful.

STARTING POINT

Discussion. What do you think of these products? Do you think any of them could be useful?

"I'd like to get my hands on one of these. It would really come in handy."

"You've got to be kidding. What a waste of money!"

Air Pollution Mask
Don't let polluted air ruin your health.

PORTA-BELLS
Wherever you are, just fill them with water and start your workout. Perfect for travel!

Riviera **Pool Chair**
Reclining seat and cup holders guarantee a great day at the pool.

1 Give shopping advice

CONVERSATION

A 🎧 CONVERSATION **SNAPSHOT**

A: I think I'd like to pick up a few souvenirs before I go back home. Any suggestions?

B: What do you have in mind?

A: Nothing in particular. Just something to help me remember my trip.

B: Well, the central market would be a good bet if you want to find a bargain.

A: Can you haggle over the prices?

B: Of course!

🎧 **Rhythm and intonation practice**

> 🎧 **Describing low prices**
> a good deal !
> a bargain !!
> a great offer !!!
> a steal !!!!

> 🎧 **Describing high prices**
> no bargain !
> a bit steep !!
> a rip-off !!!
> highway robbery !!!!

B 🎧 **Vocabulary. Shopping expressions.** Listen and practice.

browse take one's time looking at goods in a shop without necessarily wanting to buy anything
I'm not looking for anything in particular. I'm just browsing.

bargain-hunt look around for goods that one can buy cheaply or for less than their usual price
The best time to go bargain-hunting is at the end of the season when the stores have big sales.

window-shop look at goods in store windows without going inside or intending to buy them
The prices in the shops downtown are a bit steep, but I like to window-shop.

haggle / bargain discuss the amount of money one is willing to pay for something
I hate haggling over prices. / It's a great place if you like to bargain.

shop around / comparison shop go to different stores in order to compare the prices and quality of things so one can decide which to buy
I think I'll shop around first before I make up my mind. / I'd suggest you comparison shop before you buy that new computer.

C 🎧 **Listening Comprehension.** Listen to the conversations about shopping. Decide whether or not the people think the shop's prices are high. Then listen again and choose the best shopping expression to complete each statement.

Do they think the price is high?

	Yes	No	They don't say.	
1.	◯	◯	◯	They're (bargain-hunting / haggling).
2.	◯	◯	◯	They're going to (window-shop / comparison shop).
3.	◯	◯	◯	They're just (browsing / haggling).
4.	◯	◯	◯	They just want to (bargain-hunt / window-shop).
5.	◯	◯	◯	They're going to (browse / bargain).

D **Pair Work.** With a partner, fill in the duty-free price list with brand-name products you know. Then agree on a price for each product.

E **Group Work.** Compare your items and prices with other classmates'. Discuss whether or not you think the items are a good buy.

"What a steal! I'd buy that in a minute!"

"You've got to be kidding! That's highway robbery!"

Pronunciation Booster

PAGE P6
Vowel sounds

Shop Duty-free at Skymarket *and save!*

Price List

Brand Name	Product	Price

Trendy Tote Bags

Handmade Chocolates

Brand-Name Perfumes

Classic Watches

Designer Sunglasses

Compact Travel Umbrellas

CONVERSATION **STARTER** • *Now give shopping advice.*

Where are the best places to take a visitor shopping in your city or town? On your notepad, make a list.

Name of place or location	What you can buy there

IDEAS
- a shopping mall
- an open-air market
- a clothing district
- an electronics district
- a furniture district
- a boutique
- an art gallery
- a department store

Role Play. Role-play a conversation in which one of you is a visitor and the other gives shopping advice for his or her town or city. Use your notepad and the Conversation Snapshot on page 76 as a guide. Start like this: "I think I'd like to pick up a few souvenirs before I go back home."

Discussion.

1. Are you a smart shopper? Do you comparison shop or buy the first thing you see? Are you good at spotting bargains? Where do you find your best bargains?

2. What kind of shopping do you do when you're traveling? Do you shop differently when you travel from when you're at home?

Discuss your reactions to ads

A ○ GRAMMAR **SNAPSHOT.** Read the interviews and notice the passive forms of gerunds and infinitives.

What's the most touching ad you've ever seen?

**Evan Gleason, journalist
Düsseldorf, Germany**

There's a billboard for a phone company that I see every day on my way to work. It shows this elderly mother crying as she talks to her son on the phone. I'm not an emotional guy, but that ad chokes me up. It makes me think about my mom back in Los Angeles. Once in a while, we all need **to be reminded** about the important things in life.

What's the funniest ad you've ever seen?

**Mark Newcomb, engineer
Edmonton, Canada**

There's this one *really* funny TV commercial for a language school. This cat puts his head into a bowl with a goldfish swimming in it, but the fish barks like a dog and scares the cat away. Then the words "Learn another language" appear on the screen. It always cracks me up when I see it. I enjoy **having** my day **brightened** with a little laughter, even if it's just from an ad.

What's the most annoying ad you've ever seen?

**Heather Pullman, lawyer
Sydney, Australia**

That would be the soap ad they keep playing on my favorite music station. There's this one line, "Wanna get clean? Get Bream clean!" It absolutely drives me crazy. It gets on my nerves **to be forced** to listen to a dumb ad over and over again when I'm just trying to listen to music.

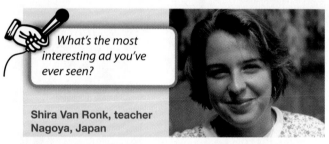

What's the most interesting ad you've ever seen?

**Shira Van Ronk, teacher
Nagoya, Japan**

Well, I know one that comes pretty close. Suntory—they're a company that produces sports drinks—they had a commercial with these amazing Chinese acrobats. The things they did just blew me away. I don't usually like commercials, but I don't mind **being entertained** by a good one.

B **Pair Work.** Use the context of the interviews to explain the meaning of each expression below.

It blows me away.   **It cracks me up.**

It gets on my nerves.   **It chokes me up.**

C **Discussion.** Do you generally find advertisements annoying or enjoyable? Why?

D **Grammar. Passive forms of gerunds and infinitives**

Use a passive form of a gerund or an infinitive to focus on an action instead of who performed the action.

Use **being** and a past participle to form a passive gerund.
  I enjoy **being entertained** by commercials.
  I resent **being forced** to watch ads before movies.
  I appreciate **not being treated** like I'm a child.

Use **to be** and a past participle to form a passive infinitive.
  I don't expect **to be told** the truth by advertisers.
  Advertisers want their products **to be remembered**.
  I was disappointed **not to be asked** to participate in the survey.

REMEMBER

• Some verbs are followed by gerunds, some by infinitives, and some by either.

• Certain adjectives are often followed by infinitives.

See page A3 in the Appendices for a complete list.

PAGE G12
For more ...

E Complete each sentence with a passive gerund or infinitive.

1. I think people enjoy (inform) .... about new products.

2. Companies want their products (advertise) .... on TV during prime time—when the most people are watching.

3. When I read an ad, I would like (tell) .... the whole truth about the product, not half-truths.

4. My sister was disappointed (not / give) .... the chance to appear in that new commercial.

F On a separate sheet of paper, rewrite each sentence. Use a passive form of a gerund or an infinitive to replace the underlined words. Do not use _by_ phrases.

REMEMBER

A <u>by</u> phrase identifies the performer of the action.

The commercial was seen by millions of people.

Example: I don't mind <u>when advertisers inform me</u> about new products.

*I don't mind **being informed** about new products.*

1. I can't stand <u>advertisers forcing me</u> to watch commercials over and over again.

2. I resent <u>one company's telling me</u> that I shouldn't buy another company's product.

3. You're lucky <u>the company is giving you</u> an opportunity to work overseas.

4. We can't tolerate <u>their calling us</u> while we're eating dinner.

GRAMMAR **EXCHANGE** • *Now discuss your reactions to ads.*

Complete the chart with ads you are familiar with. Then on a separate sheet of paper, write sentences with passive forms of gerunds or infinitives, describing how you feel about each ad in your chart.

Some types of ads
TV commercials
radio ads
magazine ads
billboards

	Name or type of product	Type of ad
an ad you find interesting		
an ad that cracks you up		
an ad that gets on your nerves		
an ad that blows you away		
an ad that chokes you up		

Describing how you feel

I like . . .	I don't like . . .
I appreciate . . .	I don't appreciate . . .
I love . . .	I can't stand . . .
I enjoy . . .	I dislike . . .
I hate . . .	I resent . . .
I prefer . . .	I miss . . .
I need . . .	I want . . .

Pair Work. Compare the ads you listed in your charts. Describe each ad and how you feel about it.

*"There's a TV commercial for shampoo that I see almost every night, and it really gets on my nerves. I can't stand **being forced** to watch it every day."*

3 Persuade someone to buy a product

A 🎧 **Vocabulary. Ways to persuade.** Listen and practice.

> **endorse** personally recommend a product in exchange for payment
>
> **promote** make sure people know about a new product in order to persuade them to buy it
>
> **imply** suggest that something is true, without saying or showing it directly
>
> **prove** show that something is definitely true, especially by providing facts, information, etc.

B **Pair Work.** Read about eight advertising techniques. Write the letter of the example that you think each technique uses. Explain your answers.

Eight techniques used by successful advertisers

1. **Provide facts and figures** ☐
   Prove the superiority of a product with statistics and objective, factual information

2. **Convince people to "join the bandwagon"** ☐
   Imply that *everyone* is using a product, and that others should too, in order to be part of the group

3. **Play on people's hidden fears** ☐
   Imply that a product will protect the user from some danger or an uncomfortable situation

4. **Play on people's patriotism** ☐
   Imply that buying a product shows love of one's country

5. **Provide "snob appeal"** ☐
   Imply that use of a product makes the customer part of an elite group

6. **Associate positive qualities with a product** ☐
   Promote a product with words and ideas having positive meanings and associations

7. **Provide testimonials** ☐
   Use a famous person or an "average consumer" to endorse a product so the consumer wants it too

8. **Manipulate people's emotions** ☐
   Use images to appeal to customers' feelings, such as love, anger, or sympathy

Source: www.entrenet.com

Examples

a. A professional soccer player recommends a particular brand of shirts.

b. A hotel chain shows a businesswoman in her room, calling home to talk to her children.

c. A soft drink manufacturer shows young people having a great time drinking its product at the beach.

d. A car manufacturer states how quickly its car can go from 0 to 100 kilometers per hour.

e. A coffee manufacturer shows people dressed in formal attire drinking its brand of coffee at an art exhibition.

f. A credit card company claims that its card is used by more people than any other card.

g. A clothing manufacturer promotes its clothes by saying they are made by and for people in this country.

h. A laundry detergent manufacturer suggests that it will be socially embarrassing if your white clothes are not *really* white.

C 🎧 **Listening Comprehension.** Listen to each ad. Then listen again. Decide which technique or techniques the advertiser is using to persuade the consumer to buy the product. Explain your answers.

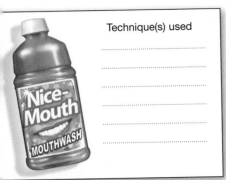

Technique(s) used
....
....
....
....
....

Technique(s) used
....
....
....
....
....

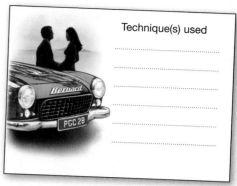

Technique(s) used
....
....
....
....
....

D **Pair Work.** Describe some ads you know and explain which techniques you think they use.

DISCUSSION **BUILDER** • *Now persuade someone to buy a product.*

Step 1. Group Work. Choose a product and create a magazine, newspaper, TV, or radio advertisement for it. Choose one or more advertising techniques to persuade your classmates to buy the product. Make notes on your notepad.

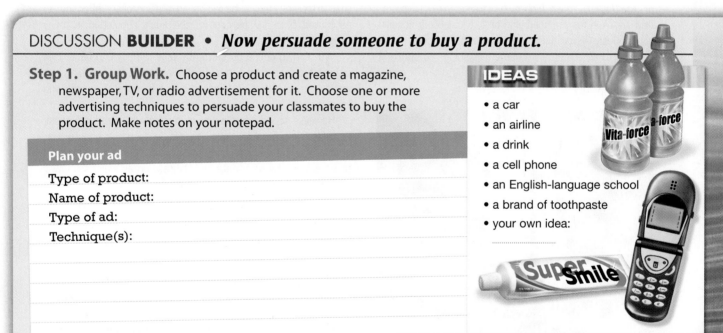

Plan your ad
Type of product:
Name of product:
Type of ad:
Technique(s):

IDEAS

- a car
- an airline
- a drink
- a cell phone
- an English-language school
- a brand of toothpaste
- your own idea:
  ....

Step 2. Discussion. Present your ad to your class. Show it, read it, or act it out. Analyze your classmates' ads and discuss which techniques were used. As a class, assign awards for these categories:

The funniest ad   The most annoying ad   The most persuasive ad   The most interesting ad   The most touching ad

Describe consumer shopping habits

A **Reading Warm-up.** Are you a careful shopper, or do you buy things on impulse?

B 🎧 **Reading.** Read the article. How is compulsive shopping a problem?

Compulsive Shopping: *The Real Cost*

Just in the last century, the way in which we consume material goods has shifted radically. For our grandparents, and some of our parents, shopping meant buying provisions to satisfy physical needs. Today, in addition to buying necessities, we shop to indulge ourselves in luxuries—high-priced gym shoes or the latest, most high-tech entertainment system. And we shop for the sheer fun of it. Most of us acquire continuously—everything from groceries to cars, from clothing to toiletries, from home furnishings to sporting equipment—and through our acquisitions, we express a sense of identity, taste, and lifestyle.

But some people go overboard. Their spending becomes excessive and often carries troubling consequences. Some people cannot resist the temptation, and very often they buy merely to acquire. This type of impulse buying can become so obsessive that people find themselves in considerable financial debt and psychological distress. Recent studies suggest that extreme impulse buying is on the increase, affecting an estimated 5 to 10 percent of the adult population in many countries.

We tend to define ourselves by what we buy and have. This often affects how we feel as well. For many, buying things on impulse is a way of avoiding or hiding feelings of anxiety and loneliness.

However, shopping as a way of dealing with internal distress is seldom effective for long. In fact, research suggests that people who consider shopping to be a priority in their lives tend to experience more anxiety and depression as well as a lower level of well-being than those who don't.

The long and short of it is this—you can't buy happiness.

Tips for Controlling Impulse Buying

- When you're just browsing and get the urge to buy something, ask yourself first if you really need it.
- Avoid sales. Spending any money on something you don't need is overspending.
- Follow the "24-hour rule." Don't buy anything new on the spot. Come back the next day if you think you really need it.
- Stick to a budget. Plan to splurge on the occasional wild purchase, but don't buy if it isn't in your budget.

Source: www.theallengroup.com

C **Understanding Meaning from Context.** Find these expressions in the article. Explain the meaning of each.

1. indulge ourselves
2. go overboard
3. resist the temptation
4. impulse buying

5. get the urge
6. overspending
7. splurge on

D **Discussion.**

1. According to the article, how have shopping habits changed over the last few generations? Do you agree?

2. Do you think compulsive shopping is a common problem? Do you know any compulsive shoppers? Give examples.

3. Do you think the tips in the article might be helpful for someone who wants to resist the temptation to overspend? What tips would *you* suggest?

DISCUSSION **BUILDER** • *Now describe consumer shopping habits.*

Step 1. Take the self-quiz. Check the statements that are true for you.

Are you a SHOPaholic?

☐ 🏷 I sometimes feel guilty about how I spend my money shopping.

☐ 🏷 When I'm feeling blue, it cheers me up to go shopping.

☐ 🏷 When I go shopping, I can't resist the temptation to buy something—I just can't come home empty-handed.

☐ 🏷 I feel uncomfortable if I haven't bought anything in a week.

☐ 🏷 When I plan to go shopping for one item I need, I frequently end up coming home with a lot of things I *don't* need.

☐ 🏷 I spend more than I have to in order to get more expensive designer names and labels.

☐ 🏷 I can't pass up a good sale—even if I don't need anything, I just have to indulge myself.

☐ 🏷 I sometimes lie to people about how much my purchases cost.

☐ 🏷 I get more pleasure out of spending money than saving money.

☐ 🏷 My shopping habits have caused problems in my personal relationships in some way.

Total the number of boxes you checked.

If your total is:

0-3 Great!
Keep up the good habits!

4-5 Not too bad!
Congratulations for admitting you're not perfect!

6-8 Uh-oh!
Sounds like trouble may be around the corner! It's time to tighten your purse strings.

9-10 Red alert!
It's time to take the bull by the horns and change some of the ways you shop and spend money.

Step 2. Discussion. Choose one of the following discussion topics and meet in small groups with other classmates who have chosen the same one.

1. Do you think most people tend to go overboard with their shopping? Explain.

2. Do you think people are too influenced by advertising? Explain.

3. Should people only spend money on things they need and never on things they don't need? Is it OK to buy on impulse sometimes? Is it OK to splurge once in a while?

Step 3. Writing. Explain your views on consumer shopping habits. In your opinion, what should people do to shop responsibly?

Writing: Explain an article you read

Writing a summary

A summary is a shortened explanation of the main ideas of an article. When writing a summary, include only the author's main points, not your own reactions or opinions. Be sure to paraphrase what the author says, instead of just copying the author's exact words.

The following guidelines will help you write a good summary:

- As you read an article, underline or highlight important points.
- Read the article again and state the main idea of each paragraph.
- Combine the main ideas to create a summary.

Some common reporting verbs used in summaries are <u>state</u>, <u>argue</u>, <u>report</u>, <u>say</u>, <u>believe</u>, <u>point out</u>, and <u>conclude</u>.

> The article states that . . .   The journalist reports that . . .
> The writer points out that . . .   The author concludes that . . .

PARAPHRASING

When you paraphrase what a person says, you say it in your *own* words.

The author: "But some people go overboard. Their spending becomes excessive and often carries troubling consequences. Some people cannot resist the temptation, and very often they buy merely to acquire."

You: *The author points out that it is difficult for some people not to buy things on impulse. They just buy anything they want.*

Step 1. Prewriting. Identifying main ideas. Read the article "Compulsive Shopping: The Real Cost" on page 82 and underline the important parts. Then read the article again and identify the main ideas below.

> Main idea of paragraph 1:
>
> Main idea of paragraph 2:
>
> Main idea of paragraph 3:
>
> Main idea of paragraph 4:

Step 2. Writing. On a separate sheet of paper, combine the main ideas to write your summary. Be sure to paraphrase what the author says, using your *own* words. Your summary should be no more than four to six sentences long.

Step 3. Self-Check.

- ☐ Is your summary a lot shorter than the original article?
- ☐ Does your summary include only the author's main ideas?
- ☐ Did you paraphrase the author's ideas?
- ☐ Did you include your opinion of the article? If so, rewrite the summary without it.

SUMMIT WEBSITE
For Unit 7 online activities, visit the *Summit* Companion Website at www.longman.com/summit.

A 🎧 **Listening Comprehension.** Listen to the conversations about prices. Then read the statements and listen again. Circle the phrase that best completes each statement, according to what the people say.

1. **a.** The woman thinks the price of the first vase is (a bit steep / a real bargain).
   The man thinks it's (a steal / a rip-off).

   b. The woman thinks the second vase is (a steal / a good deal).
   The man thinks it's (a rip-off / no bargain).

2. **a.** The woman thinks the exercise bike from Freeman's was (a great offer / a rip-off).
   The man thinks it was (no bargain / a steal).

   b. The woman thinks the price of the bike from Mason's is (a bit steep / a great deal).
   The man thinks it's (a better offer / no deal).

3. **a.** The man thinks the price of the necklace is (a bit steep / no deal).
   The woman thinks it's (pretty steep / a bargain).

   b. The man thinks the earrings are (a good deal / a rip-off).
   The woman thinks they're (a great deal / no bargain).

B Complete each statement with your *own* ideas.

Example: *Watching old Charlie Chaplin movies always* cracks me up.

1. _____ cracks me up.

2. _____ blows me away.

3. _____ chokes me up.

4. _____ gets on my nerves.

C Complete the statements with passive forms of gerunds or infinitives.

1. I don't recall _____ any information.
   (send)

2. They want _____ more time for the project.
   (give)

3. She arranged _____ to the airport.
   (take)

4. I was disappointed _____ the news.
   (tell)

5. He risked _____ from his job.
   (fire)

6. We were delighted _____ to the wedding.
   (invite)

D On a separate sheet of paper, answer the questions in your *own* way.

1. What kinds of things do you like to splurge on?

2. Have you ever gone a little overboard buying something? Explain.

3. What can't you resist the temptation to do? Why?

UNIT 8

Family Trends

UNIT GOALS

1 Describe family trends
2 Discuss parent–teen issues
3 Compare generations
4 Describe care for the elderly

A **Topic Preview.** Look at the two cartoons about families. Then answer the questions with a partner.

"Because this family isn't ready to hold democratic elections—that's why!"

1. Who do you think was speaking before the father spoke? What do you think was said?

2. Is your family a "democracy"? How do decisions get made?

3. What didn't the father have when he was young that the son has now? Do you think the father has a good point, or is he being ridiculous?

4. In your family, is there a "generation gap" between older and younger family members? Explain.

"You have it easy. When I was your age, I had to walk all the way across the room to change the channel."

B **Discussion.** Do you think the cartoons are funny? Do you think they portray typical families? Why or why not?

C 🎧 **Sound Bites.** Read and listen to a conversation about relationships.

Sam

Margaret

TERESA: Did you hear that Sam and Margaret got back together?
BETTINA: Wow! I didn't even know they'd split up! It shows you how out of touch I am.
TERESA: Well, they had this major falling out about two months ago, and they separated. But it looks like they've patched things up.
BETTINA: Good. They're a nice couple. I hope things work out for them.
TERESA: Me too. So, how's *your* family?
BETTINA: Not bad, but we've been having some trouble with our son.
TERESA: Really? What kind of trouble?
BETTINA: Well, he's been acting up in school. You know, talking back to his teachers, not doing his homework.
TERESA: Eric? I can't believe it! He's always been so well-behaved!
BETTINA: Well, I told him he's grounded until he shapes up. No movies, no games, no trips to the mall.
TERESA: Smart move. Eric's a good kid, but you don't want him to turn into a troublemaker.

D **In Other Words.** Read the conversation again. With a partner, use the context of the conversation to figure out what each of the expressions means.

1. They **got back together**.
2. They **split up**.
3. They **had a falling out**.
4. They **patched things up**.
5. Things **didn't work out**.
6. My kids have been **acting up**.
7. Don't **talk back**!
8. Your son is so **well-behaved**.
9. He'd better **shape up**!
10. That kid is such **a troublemaker**.

E **Discussion.** Do you think grounding Eric is a smart move? Why or why not? In your opinion, what's the best way to handle or discipline a teenager who has been acting up?

STARTING **POINT**

Pair Work. Choose one of the topics. Tell your partner about a time you . . .

had a difference of opinion with someone from another generation.

had a falling out with a friend, a family member, or a colleague.

helped patch things up for someone else.

1 *Describe family trends*

A 🎧 GRAMMAR **SNAPSHOT.** Read the information in the brochure and notice the use of comparatives.

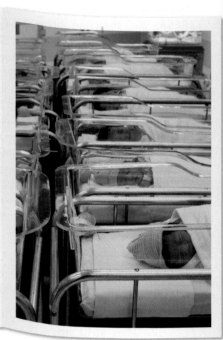

Falling Birthrates

Current trends show the size of families is changing, impacting societies worldwide. Women are marrying later, and couples are waiting longer to have children. And **the longer** couples wait to have children, **the fewer** children they have.

Two key factors that impact family size are the education and the employment of women. Studies show that **the more** education women get, **the smaller** families they have. Moreover, **the longer** women stay in school, **the better** their opportunities for employment. Working women are less likely to marry young and have large families.

In addition to the falling birthrate, there is a rising life expectancy. With people living **longer and longer**, families are going to have to face the challenges posed by an aging population. **The longer** people live, **the more** care they require. Traditionally, children have cared for their elderly parents at home. However, **the more** the birthrate falls, **the harder** the future may be for the elderly. With fewer children, families may find it **more and more** difficult to care for their older members.

Source: United Nations Statistics Division

B **Discussion.**

1. According to the brochure, what factors explain why more couples are having fewer children?

2. Why do you think populations are living longer? What problems does a larger elderly population pose?

C **Grammar. Repeated comparatives and double comparatives**

Repeated comparatives are used to describe actions and things that are increasing or decreasing.
The birthrate is getting **lower and lower**.
By the end of the twentieth century, couples were waiting **longer and longer** to marry.
More and more people are marrying later.
Fewer and fewer children are leaving school.
It's becoming **more and more** difficult.

Double comparatives are used to describe a cause-and-effect process.
The more education women get, **the later** they marry. [Women are getting more education, so they're marrying later.]
The less children studied, **the more slowly** they learned. [Children studied less, so they learned more slowly.]

NOTE: When _be_ is used in double comparatives, it is sometimes omitted.
The better the quality of health care (is), **the higher** the life expectancy (is).

BE CAREFUL! Don't use continuous verb forms in double comparatives.
The longer couples **wait** to have children, the fewer children they **have**.
NOT The longer couples ~~are waiting~~ to have children, the fewer ~~they're having~~.

Grammar Booster

PAGE G13
For more ...

D Complete each statement logically, using double comparatives.

1. _____ people are when they marry, _____ children they have.
   (old) (few)

2. _____ the life expectancy, _____ the elderly population is.
   (high) (large)

3. _____ people work, _____ they are.
   (hard) (successful)

4. _____ the quality of health care is, _____ the death rate.
   (good) (low)

5. _____ the country is, _____ the life expectancy.
   (developed) (low)

6. _____ women are when they have children, _____ they are to get a higher education.
   (young) (likely)

E 🎧 **Listening Comprehension.** Listen to three people talking about trends in marriage and family life. Then listen again and complete each statement, according to what the speaker implies, using double comparatives.

1. _____ education mothers get, _____ medical care they receive.

2. _____ couples date, _____ they marry.

3. _____ children stay in school, _____ their life expectancy.

GRAMMAR **EXCHANGE** • *Now describe family trends.*

Pair Work. Use repeated comparatives to discuss the ways families are changing in your country.

"People are getting married later and later."

IDEAS

- birthrate
- life expectancy
- age at marriage
- health
- education
- income
- employment opportunities
- generational differences

Writing. On a separate sheet of paper, write about the impact of the changes you've discussed. Use repeated comparatives and double comparatives.

> In the last few decades, family size has declined. Fewer and fewer people are having big families, so their standard of living is higher. The higher the standard of living is, the healthier the population.

Discussion. In small groups, compare the trends you've identified. How will these changes impact families in the future?

"It seems like more and more people are having fewer children. This could be a problem later because...."

2 *Discuss parent–teen issues*

A ⌒ CONVERSATION **SNAPSHOT**

A: What do you think parents should do if their
teenage kids start smoking?

B: Well, I hate to say it, but there's not much they can do.

A: Why's that?

B: Well, teenagers are out of the house most of the day,
so parents can't control everything they do.

A: I suppose. But they can ground them if they
don't shape up.

⌒ **Rhythm and intonation practice**

⌒ **Examples of bad behavior**
- acting up at school
- staying out late without permission
- being rude and disrespectful
- becoming a troublemaker

B ⌒ **Vocabulary. Describing parent and teen behavior.** Listen and practice.

Parents can sometimes be . . .

(too) strict

They set a lot of restrictions and
expect kids to obey rules.

(too) lenient

They let their kids have or do anything
they want.

overprotective

They worry too much about their kids.

Teenagers can sometimes be . . .

rebellious

They refuse to follow rules and do the
opposite of what is expected of them.

spoiled

They expect to have or do whatever
they want.

disrespectful

They are rude to adults and think what
adults say is not important.

C Correct the adjective in each of the following statements.

1. Parents who always allow their teenage children to stay out late are *overprotective*.

2. Teenagers who demand that their parents buy everything they ask for are *rebellious*.

3. When parents never let their children do things because they are afraid that their children
will get sick or hurt, they are being *strict*.

4. When a teen gets a tattoo against a parent's wishes, we say that he or she is *disrespectful*.

5. Parents who make their teenage children clean their rooms every day are *lenient*.

6. Teens who don't listen to adults and often talk back are *spoiled*.

D 🎧 **Listening Comprehension.** Listen to the conversations about parent and teen behavior. Then listen again and determine which adjective from the vocabulary best completes each statement.

1. She thinks he's ....

2. She thinks he's acting ....

3. He thinks she's ....

4. He's angry because she's being ....

5. He thinks she's ....

6. She criticizes him for being ....

E **Discussion.** Can you identify with any of the people in the listening? Are any of the speakers like anyone you know? Explain.

CONVERSATION **STARTER** • *Now discuss parent–teen issues.*

Pair Work. Discuss and complete the survey. Compare your ideas. Give specific examples to support your answers.

Circle the rating that most closely expresses your opinion.

1 = completely agree   2 = somewhat agree, depending on the circumstances   3 = completely disagree

PARENTS		Me	My partner
	Parents should let kids make their own mistakes. Being overprotective with children makes kids less responsible.	1 2 3	1 2 3
	It's OK to give in to kids' demands sometimes in order to "keep the peace."	1 2 3	1 2 3
	Parents should include their children in family decision-making. After all, kids' opinions are important, too.	1 2 3	1 2 3
	It's a good idea for parents to use physical punishment to discipline their children. If parents aren't strict, their kids will become troublemakers.	1 2 3	1 2 3
	Your own idea:		1 2 3

TEENS		Me	My partner
	Teenagers don't always have to obey their parents. Sometimes it's OK to say "no."	1 2 3	1 2 3
	Teenagers shouldn't have to help around the house. They already have enough to do with their schoolwork.	1 2 3	1 2 3
	Teenagers are mature enough to make their own decisions. They shouldn't have to ask permission for everything.	1 2 3	1 2 3
	Teenagers have a right to privacy. They shouldn't have to tell their parents about everything they do.	1 2 3	1 2 3
	Your own idea:		1 2 3

Role Play. Role-play a conversation in which you discuss parent or teen behavior. Use the Conversation Snapshot on page 90 as a guide. Start like this:

"What do you think parents should do if   **OR**   "What do you think kids should do their teenage kids . . . ?"   if their parents . . . ?"

Discussion. If you could give parents one piece of advice, what would it be? If you could give teenagers one piece of advice, what would it be?

3 *Compare generations*

A 🎧 **Word Skills.** Transforming verbs and adjectives into nouns

common noun endings	nouns		common noun endings	nouns
-ation -tion -ssion	expect → expectation explain → explanation frustrate → frustration permit → permission		-ness	fair → fairness rebellious → rebelliousness selfish → selfishness strict → strictness
-ment	develop → development involve → involvement		-ity	generous → generosity mature → maturity mobile → mobility secure → security
-y	courteous → courtesy difficult → difficulty			
-ility	responsible → responsibility reliable → reliability capable → capability dependable → dependability		-ance -ence	important → importance independent → independence lenient → lenience obedient → obedience

NOTE: Sometimes internal spelling changes occur when a noun ending is added to a verb or an adjective.

Pronunciation Booster

PAGE P7
Stress placement

B Circle all the words that are nouns. Check in a dictionary if you are not sure about the meaning of a word.

1. dependency   depend   dependence   dependent

2. impatient   impatience   impatiently

3. confidence   confident   confide   confidently

4. unfair   unfairness   unfairly

5. consider   consideration   considerate   considerately

6. closeness   close   closely

7. different   difference   differentiate   differentiation

8. happily   happy   happiness

9. attraction   attract   attractive   attractiveness

Vilnius, the capital of Lithuania

C 🎧 **Listening Comprehension.** Listen to Part 1 of a man's description of the generation gap in his family. Then answer the questions.

1. In terms of family size, how did Rimas grow up differently from his parents?

2. Why does Rimas's father think teenagers nowadays have more problems than when he was growing up?

D 🎧 Listen to Part 1 again. Then complete each statement.

1. Rimas grew up in _____, but his parents grew up in _____.

2. Rimas's extended family includes _____ aunts and uncles on his mother's side.

3. When Rimas's mother was growing up, every evening she ate dinner _____. However, when Rimas and his sister were kids, they sometimes had to eat _____.

Rimas Vilkas

E 🎧 Now listen to Part 2. Then listen again and complete the chart by describing the differences between the two generations. Compare your chart with a partner's.

How are they different?		
	Rimas's parents' generation	Rimas's generation
career choices		
mobility		
influences from other cultures		
age at marriage and childbearing		
work experience		
closeness of family		

F Discussion.

1. Why do Rimas's parents worry about him and the future? Why do you think parents always worry about their children?

2. In what ways is the Vilkas's family story similar to or different from yours?

DISCUSSION **BUILDER** • *Now compare generations.*

Step 1. Pair Work. Compare your parents' generation with your generation. Write your ideas on your notepad. Discuss them with a partner.

	My parents' generation	**My generation**
music		
style of clothes		
hairstyles / facial hair		
attitude toward elders		
family responsibility		
language (idioms, slang)		
marriage and childbearing		
values and beliefs		
other:		

Step 2. Discussion.

1. In what ways is your generation most different from your parents' generation? What do you like best or respect most about your parents' generation?

2. What contributions do you think your generation will make to the next generation? How do you think the next generation will differ from yours?

4 Describe care for the elderly

A **Reading Warm-up.** In previous generations, how have older family members traditionally been cared for in your country?

B 🎧 **Reading.** Read the article. What impact has China's one-child policy had on care for the elderly?

Uncertain Future for China's Elderly

Due to a sharp increase in its aging population, China faces new social problems in the future, according to a recent report from the Chinese Academy of Sciences. In China today, the elderly—people aged 60 or older—make up about 11 percent of the population. However, according to United Nations statistics, by 2050 the number of elderly will increase to more than 31 percent. If this trend continues, the elderly could eventually outnumber young people—a dramatic change for China.

While lower birthrates and higher life expectancies are causing similar population shifts in many countries, this transformation is happening faster in China due to the strict one-child policy introduced in 1979. Under this policy, couples can have only one child. The policy's purpose was to stop China's burgeoning population from growing too fast. It created a generation of "only children" growing up without brothers or sisters who can share the burden of caring for elderly family members.

According to Chinese tradition, the elderly have always been honored and respected by the young; for generations, parents and grandparents have relied on their children to care for them in old age. But today an increasing number of single young adults face the

difficult situation of caring for both their parents and their grandparents. This phenomenon is known as a 4-2-1 family: For every *one* child, there are *two* parents and *four* grandparents to look after. Breaking with tradition, many young adults who can afford it are beginning to transfer the responsibility of looking after their elderly relatives to private nursing homes. This change in attitude is causing some conflict and anger between generations.

The aging of China's population will have a big impact on the country's future. The less the old can depend on the young, the more they may have to depend on the government. In one attempt to deal with this problem, the government has started a national lottery to raise money for elder care. However, it may still need to create more resources to care for its graying population.

China's one-child families have had an unexpected effect on care for the elderly.

Source: Adapted from the *Beijing Times* (August 21, 2002)

C **Discussion.**

1. Describe how China's population is changing. What is causing those changes?

2. According to the article, what challenges are China's young people facing today?

3. How may elder care in China differ in the future from the traditions of the past?

DISCUSSION **BUILDER** • *Now describe care for the elderly.*

Step 1. Pair Work. Discuss the statements and check those you think are true about care for the elderly in your country.

- ☐ Most elderly people are adequately cared for.
- ☐ The way the elderly are cared for has been changing.
- ☐ The elderly usually live with younger family members.
- ☐ The elderly usually live in their own homes or apartments.
- ☐ The elderly usually live in special nursing homes.
- ☐ The government makes sure the elderly have affordable care.
- ☐ Younger people accept care for elderly relatives as their responsibility.
- ☐ Older people generally prefer not to socialize with younger people.
- ☐ Other: ....

Step 2. Pair Work. Read each case study. Discuss the challenges each person is facing and recommend solutions.

Ingrid is divorced and has three young daughters. Her mother died years ago, and her seventy-five-year-old father can no longer take care of himself. He often forgets things. She worries that he might get hurt.

Robert's parents, who live in another city, are in their eighties. They continue to have a full social life, and they still enjoy traveling with organized tours. But they are not as strong as they used to be and need help with cooking and cleaning.

Nick is married and has two teenage children. His mother just turned seventy-nine and lives alone. Nick and his family live in a very small apartment with two bedrooms. He and his wife both work overtime, putting in long hours in order to make ends meet. Nick is concerned about his mother's health and well-being.

Step 3. Discussion. How do you think the elderly will be cared for by the time you are old? How would *you* like to be cared for? Describe the ideal situation for elder care. Use language from the checklist in Step 1.

Step 4. Writing. Write a description for a visitor to your country of how the elderly are cared for.

Writing: Describe your relationship with a family member

Avoiding comma splices and run-on sentences

Note two common errors that writers often make when joining two sentences.

Comma splice (connecting two sentences with a comma and no conjunction)
INCORRECT: My grandmother taught me how to bake, now I know how to make great cookies.

Run-on sentence (connecting sentences without using punctuation)
INCORRECT: My grandmother taught me how to bake however I never do.

To correct a comma splice or a run-on sentence, choose one of the following:

- Use a period and capitalize the following word.

  My grandmother taught me how to bake. Now I know how to make great cookies.
  My grandmother taught me how to bake. However, I never do.

- Use a semicolon.

  My grandmother taught me how to bake; now I know how to make great cookies.
  My grandmother taught me how to bake; however, I never do.

- Use a comma and a coordinating conjunction.

  My grandmother taught me how to bake, and now I know how to make great cookies.
  My grandmother taught me how to bake, but I never do.

Coordinating conjunctions

and	for	or	yet
but	nor	so	

ERROR CORRECTION Correct the three error

Everyone tells me I am a great cook however, everything I know about baking I learned from my grandmother. I always helped my grandmother when she baked we made cookies, cakes, pies, and breads together. I even had more fun baking than eating the food! At first I wondered how she was able to put various ingredients together without measuring cups and written recipes with time, I also learned the tricks. When my grandmother died, she left me all her baking and cooking equipment and many years of wonderful memories.

Step 1. Prewriting. "Freewriting" to generate ideas.

Writing quickly without stopping is one way to generate ideas. First, choose a family relationship you would like to write about. Then, write anything that comes to mind for five minutes. Write quickly and do not worry about spelling, punctuation, etc. Finally, read what you wrote. Select some of the ideas from your freewriting and organize them logically.

> My grandparents
> —in their seventies
> —always help me
> —grandfather likes to fish
> —grandmother loves when I visit

Step 2. Writing.
On a separate sheet of paper, write a paragraph about the relationship you chose. Include a topic sentence that expresses your main idea. Avoid comma splices and run-on sentences.

Step 3. Self-Check.

☐ Did you write any run-on sentences? Comma splices? If so, correct them.
☐ Do all the sentences support the topic sentence?
☐ Is the paragraph interesting? What could you add to make it more interesting?

SUMMIT WEBSITE
For Unit 8 online activities, visit the
Summit Companion Website at
www.longman.com/summit.

A 🎧 **Listening Comprehension.** Listen to the conversations about generational issues. Then listen to each conversation again and complete each statement with the correct comparative.

1. Philip is spending .... time on his homework.
   a. more and more   **b.** less and less

2. ...., the more her mother worries.
   a. The later Sandi stays out   **b.** The older Sandi gets

3. The stricter Jill's father gets, ... she becomes.
   a. the more rebellious   **b.** the more spoiled

4. The older the sisters get, ...
   a. the smarter they become   **b.** the more they appreciate their parents

B Write the adjective that best describes the behavior in each statement.

1. Mark's parents don't allow him to watch more than two hours of TV a day, but most of his friends can watch as much as they want. He feels that his parents are ....

2. Karen has a closet full of expensive clothes, yet she always complains about not having anything to wear. Her parents usually buy her whatever she wants. A lot of people think Karen is ....

3. Even though she has had her driver's license for a year and a half, Marissa's parents worry about her driving at night. They say that it's too dangerous, but Marissa thinks they're just being ....

4. When Clyde's grandfather asked him to turn down the volume on his CD player, he ignored him and continued to listen to his music. Clyde's grandfather thought this was very ....

5. Rodney and Carolyn believe parents don't need to be so concerned about their children. They rarely set rules for their kids. Carolyn's sister thinks this is a bad idea. She feels they're ....

6. Deanna wears clothing that her parents find shocking. She also has friends that her parents don't approve of. Her mother wishes she weren't so ....

C Correct the part of speech of any of the incorrect underlined words.

1. Teenagers were given a lot more <u>responsibility</u> when I was young.

2. I think teenagers today lack the <u>mature</u> to make decisions for themselves.

3. The main reason young people are rebellious today is <u>selfishness</u>.

4. If kids today were taught about <u>courteous</u>, they would be better behaved.

5. There's no question that teenagers today demand more <u>independent</u> than they did fifty years ago.

6. It's important to be involved in your child's <u>development</u>.

7. Young people have a lot more <u>mobile</u> than they did several generations ago.

8. It seems like there's a lot more <u>rebellious</u> among teenagers today.

UNIT GOALS

1 Speculate about the out-of-the-ordina
2 Present a theory about a past event
3 Discuss how believable a story is
4 Evaluate the trustworthiness of news sources

A **Topic Preview.** Take the quiz with a partner and discuss your answers.

The World's Easiest Quiz . . .
or is it?

How long did the Hundred Years' War last? The answer *has* to be a hundred years, right? Well, the answer may not be what you think. Take a stab at this quiz and see how many answers you can guess correctly. Then check your answers below.

1. How long did the Hundred Years' War in Western Europe last?
a. 100 years   c. 50 years
b. 116 years   d. 200 years

2. Which country makes Panama hats?
a. Panama
b. the Philippines
c. Ecuador
d. Italy

3. From which animals do we get catgut for violin strings?
a. cats   c. sharks
b. sheep   d. dogs

4. The former U.S.S.R. used to celebrate the October Revolution in which month?
a. October   c. December
b. November   d. June

5. What is a camel hair paintbrush made of?
a. camel hair   c. cat hair
b. squirrel hair   d. human hair

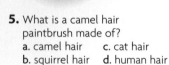

6. The Canary Islands in the Atlantic Ocean are named after what animal?
a. the canary   c. the dog
b. the cat   d. the camel

7. What was King George VI of England's first name?
a. George   c. Jose
b. Charles   d. Albert

8. What color is a male purple finch?
a. dark purple   c. sky blue
b. crimson red   d. white

9. What country do Chinese gooseberries come from?
a. China   c. Sweden
b. Japan   d. New Zealand

10. How long did the Thirty Years' War in Central Europe last?
a. 30 years   c. 20 years
b. 40 years   d. 100 years

SCORING

1–2 correct Hmm . . . Maybe you need to work on your guessing skills!

3–5 correct Not a bad job at guessing! Or did you already know a few of the answers?

6–10 correct Either you're a great guesser, or you're a real scholar!

ANSWERS: 1. b. 116 years (The war ran from 1337 to 1453, but with interruptions.) **2. c.** Ecuador (In the 16th century, the hats were shipped through the Panama Canal.) **3. b.** sheep (Catgut comes from the German *kitgut*, a type of violin.) **4. b.** November (Russians used to use the Julian calendar, which was different from the Gregorian calendar by 13 days.) **5. b.** squirrel hair (The brush was named after its inventor, whose surname was Camel.) **6. c.** the dog (The word canary comes from the Latin *Insularia Canaria—Island of the Dogs*.) **7. d.** Albert (British kings usually take new names.) **8. b.** crimson red (This is the only "red finch" with purple on its chest.) **9. d.** New Zealand (New Zealanders renamed them kiwi fruit to avoid confusion.) **10. a.** 30 years, of course! (The war lasted from 1618 to 1648.)

B **Discussion.** Did you have a particular reason for each of the answers you chose? Did you just take "wild guesses," or did you use "the process of elimination"? Which method do you think works better? Why?

C 🎧 **Sound Bites.** Read and listen to a conversation about a well-known mystery.

VICTOR: I saw the most fascinating TV program about Bigfoot last night.
PATTY: Bigfoot? Don't tell me you buy that story!
VICTOR: You're such a skeptic! Who's to say those things don't exist? How else would you explain all those sightings over the years?
PATTY: Could've been gorillas.
VICTOR: In the U.S.? I don't think so. There's no question—Bigfoot is real.
PATTY: Get out of here! There's no such thing as Bigfoot. You have such a wild imagination!
VICTOR: You'd change your mind if you'd seen that program.
PATTY: The only way I'd change my mind is if I saw one of them with my own two eyes. Seeing is believing, as far as I'm concerned.

Bigfoot
Many people claim to have seen a hairy, human-like creature—called "Bigfoot"—in the western mountains of the United States. In 2004, Bob Heironimus admitted that he dressed in a costume for this famous 1967 image.

D **In Other Words.** Read the conversation again. With a partner, explain the meaning of each of the following statements.

1. "Don't tell me you buy that story!"
2. "You're such a skeptic!"
3. "There's no question—Bigfoot is real."
4. "Get out of here!"
5. "You have such a wild imagination!"
6. "Seeing is believing."

STARTING POINT

Pair Work. Read about these two mysteries. How possible is it that each is true? Discuss your opinions with a partner.

The Loch Ness Monster
For centuries, people have reported sightings of a very large, unfamiliar animal living in the deepest lake in the United Kingdom — Scotland's Loch Ness.

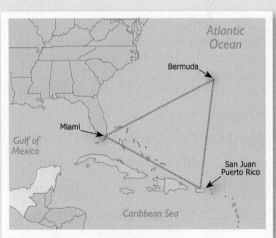

The Bermuda Triangle
Over several centuries, in a triangular area of the Caribbean Sea, numerous ships have mysteriously disappeared—never to be seen again. Many believe that there is something about that area that causes ships simply to disappear into thin air.

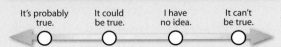

It's probably true. | It could be true. | I have no idea. | It can't be true.

It's probably true. | It could be true. | I have no idea. | It can't be true.

1 *Speculate about the out-of-the-ordinary*

A ⌒ CONVERSATION **SNAPSHOT**

A: I wonder where Stacey is. She said she'd be here by ten.

B: Do you think something happened?

A: Beats me.

B: Well, I'm sure it's nothing. I'll bet she's stuck in traffic.

A: You're probably right.

B: Why else would she be late?

A: I can't imagine.

⌒ **Rhythm and intonation practice**

> ⌒ **Ways to say "I don't know."**
>
> Beats me.
> I can't imagine.
> I don't have a clue.
> I have no idea.
> Your guess is as good as mine.
> You got me.
> Who knows?

B Grammar. Indirect speech with modals

REMEMBER: When a reporting verb is in a past form, the verb in the indirect speech statement usually changes or "backshifts."

"I **went** to the store." → She said [that] she **had gone** to the store.

PAGE G14
For more ...

Some modals also backshift in indirect speech.

"I'**ll** be there by six." → I said [that] I **would** be there by six.
"You **must** come on time." → She said [that] they **had to** come on time.
"You **have to*** pay in cash." → They told me [that] I **had to** pay in cash.

Some modals don't backshift in indirect speech.

"You **should** hurry." → She told him [that] he **should** hurry.
"He **might** call tonight." → He said [that] he **might** call tonight.

Perfect modals never backshift in indirect speech.

"We **must have** forgotten." → He said [that] they **must have** forgotten.

Modals that backshift	Modals that don't backshift
will → would	would → would
can → could	could → could
may → might	might → might
must → had to	should → should
have to → had to	ought to → ought to

> **REMEMBER**
>
> In indirect speech, pronouns and possessives change in order to preserve the speaker's meaning.
>
> "**My** brother got **me** a gift." → She said [that] **her** brother had gotten **her** a gift.

* <u>Have to</u> is not a true modal, but it is often referred to as a "modal-like expression."

C Change each sentence from direct to indirect speech.

1. He told me, "You shouldn't worry if I arrive a little late." ....

2. He said, "Students must arrive fifteen minutes early." ....

3. "Jack may have gotten lost," he said. ....

4. "They might have forgotten their luggage," she said. ....

5. She told me, "I'll call you as soon as I get there." ....

6. She told us, "I may have to cancel the meeting." ....

7. He told me, "I'll come early." ....

8. "You ought to phone first," she told me. ....

very certain		almost certain	
Clearly It's obvious } he's not coming. There's no question		Most likely Probably } someone found it. I'll bet	

somewhat certain		not certain	
I guess I imagine } she's lost. I suppose		Maybe It's possible } he forgot. It could be	

CONVERSATION **STARTER** • *Now speculate about the out-of-the-ordinary.*

Pair Work. Choose one of the out-of-the-ordinary situations below or create your own. Discuss and speculate about the situation. On a separate sheet of paper, use the vocabulary to write four sentences about the situation in which you are very certain, almost certain, somewhat certain, and not certain.

I'll bet the elevator isn't working.

It's 9:30, and your teacher hasn't arrived yet for your 9:00 class.

You're trying to take the elevator downstairs to get some lunch. You've been waiting for the elevator for over ten minutes.

You expected a package to arrive on Monday. It's Friday, and it still hasn't come.

Role Play. Role-play the situation you chose or choose another one, speculating about what you think happened. Use the Conversation Snapshot on page 100 as a guide. Start like this: "I wonder …."

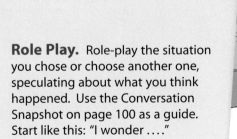

You go to your favorite restaurant. The lights are on, but the doors are locked, and there's no one inside.

2 Present a theory about a past event

GRAMMAR

A 🎧 GRAMMAR **SNAPSHOT.** Read the articles and notice the use of perfect modals in the passive voice.

THE STONE BALLS OF COSTA RICA

One of the strangest mysteries in archaeology was discovered in the Diquis Delta of Costa Rica. Since the 1930s, hundreds of stone balls have been found, ranging in size from a few centimeters to over two meters in diameter. Some weigh as much as 16 tons. Almost all of them are made of hard stone and are clearly made by human hands. Nobody knows for sure, but it's believed that the balls **could have been made** by the ancestors of native peoples who lived in the region at the time of the Spanish conquest. But what they **might have been used** for is a total mystery.

Source: www.world-mysteries.com

An Explosion in Tunguska

At 7:17 A.M. on June 30, 1908, an explosion of catastrophic proportions occurred in the forests of Tunguska in northern Siberia, 3,540 kilometers east of Moscow. All over Europe there were reports of strange colors in the sky. It was impossible to investigate the incident because it was so far from where people lived at the time. Most scientists assume that the area **must have been struck** by a huge meteorite. But there are some researchers who claim that the area **couldn't have been hit** by a meteorite because there was no evidence of a crater—the type of hole a meteorite would have caused.

Source: en.wikipedia.org

B **Discussion.** Are you familiar with either of these stories? Have you heard about any other similar mysteries? Describe them.

C **Grammar.** Perfect modals in the passive voice for speculating about the past

You can use **may**, **might**, **could**, **must**, or **had to** to speculate with different degrees of certainty about the past. Use the passive voice if the performer of the action is unknown or if you want to focus on the receiver of the action.

not certain	The dinosaurs **might** (or **may**) **have been killed** by a meteor. The trees **could have been destroyed** by a fire. The gold figures **might not** (or **may not**) **have been lost**.
almost certain	The stone balls **must have been moved** using animals. The drawings **must not have been discovered** until later.
very certain	The crater **had to have been caused** by a meteorite. The trees **couldn't** (or **can't**) **have been burned** in a fire.

Short responses with perfect modals in the passive voice

Is it possible they were killed by a meteorite?	They **may have been**.
Do you think they were made by hand?	They **had to have been**.
I wonder if they could have just been lost.	They **couldn't have been**.
Could they have been stolen?	They **might have been**.

D Complete each conversation about these sensational headlines, using perfect modals in the passive voice. Make sure each conversation makes sense.

Harvard Professor Claims Egyptian Pyramids Built by Aliens from Outer Space

1. **A:** Do you think the pyramids .... by aliens from outer space?
   B: No way! They .... I just don't believe that!

New Zealand Scientist Argues Dinosaurs Killed by Giant Tsunami

2. **A:** Do you believe the dinosaurs .... by a giant tsunami?
   B: They .... It might explain how they all disappeared so quickly.

SHOCKING NEW REVELATION:
Artist van Gogh was actually murdered by brother

3. **A:** Do you think van Gogh .... by his brother?
   B: Oh, come on! He .... Everyone knows he killed himself.

Woman Attacked by Tiger While Shopping in London

4. **A:** Do you think someone .... by a tiger in London?
   B: Get out of here! That story .... made up!
   A: I guess you're right. It ....

Pronunciation Booster

PAGE P9
Reduction and linking

GRAMMAR **EXCHANGE** • *Now present a theory about a past event.*

Pair Work. Read about each mystery and the theories explaining it. Which theory do you think is the most possible? Speculate with perfect modals in the passive voice when possible.

Stonehenge

This formation in southern England was built over 3,000 years ago. The stones were brought from mountains far away, but no one knows for sure how the stones were carried or put into place. The purpose for the stone formation is unknown.

Theories:
a. It was used as a type of calendar.
b. It was used for religious ceremonies.
c. It wasn't made or used by people at all— it was formed naturally.

The Nazca Lines

These shapes were carved into the earth in Peru more than 1,500 years ago. However, the people who made them could not have seen what they were carving—the figures can only be seen from an airplane. No one knows how they were made.

Theories:
a. They were carved by ancient people, who used small drawings to design them.
b. With the help of airplanes, they were carved in 1927, right before they were supposedly "discovered."
c. They were created by aliens, who were able to see them from their spaceships.

Atlantis

Around 350 B.C.E., the Greek philosopher Plato wrote about a lost continent called "Atlantis." He describes this advanced civilization in great detail. Researchers argue whether the story is true or comes from Plato's imagination.

Theories:
a. It was a real community established by the Greeks that was destroyed by an earthquake and sank into the ocean.
b. It was a real place discovered by ancient explorers. We know it today as Iceland.
c. Plato was tricked into believing the story by one of his students.

Presentation. Choose one of the mysteries. Present the theory that you think best explains the mystery and tell the class why you believe it.

> *"I believe the stones **may have been used** for religious purposes. That's what makes the most sense to me."*

3 Discuss how believable a story is

A 🎧 Word Skills. Using adjectives with the suffix -able

believable can be accepted as true because it seems possible
The story he told seems believable. He backed it up with a lot of details.

debatable not easy to prove because more than one explanation is possible
The cause of the explosion is debatable; experts still disagree.

provable can be shown to be definitely true
I don't think your theory will be provable, unless clear evidence can be found.

questionable uncertain, but more likely to be untrue
Her convincing account of the events makes his version highly questionable.

unsolvable impossible to prove
This mystery may be unsolvable. Everyone who saw what happened is no longer alive.

B Complete each statement, using an adjective with the suffix -able. Use each adjective only once.

1. His story is really .... I doubt that those things could have really happened.

2. I think she's telling the truth. Her description of the events sounds very .... to me.

3. It is highly .... whether "lie-detector" testing should be used as evidence. Experts continue to argue about what the test results really mean.

4. What happened to the dinosaurs is not really .... There is nothing that can show with certainty what really happened.

5. The mystery of what happened to the famous U.S. pilot Amelia Earhart is most likely .... since her body and the plane have never been found.

C 🎧 Listening Comprehension. Listen to Part 1 of a historical mystery. What happened to the Russian royal family? What's mysterious about this event?

Russia's Royal Family: An Enduring Mystery

St. Petersburg
Ural Mountains
Yekaterinburg
R U S S I A

Anna Anderson, who claimed to have been Anastasia

Russia's last royal family: Czar Nicholas II and Empress Alexandra with their children, Olga, Maria, Anastasia, Alexei, and Tatiana.

D 🎧 Now listen to Part 2. What happened in 1991, and what facts did it seem to prove? Why is it still a mystery?

LISTENING

E Complete each statement, according to the listening. Listen to Part 2 again if necessary.

1. The czar's son, Alexei, ...
   a. might have been executed with the rest of the family
   b. must have been executed with the rest of the family

2. Researchers believed that five of the nine bodies discovered in 1991 ....
   a. couldn't have been the royal family
   b. had to have been the royal family

3. Anna Anderson, who claimed to be Anastasia, ...
   a. couldn't have been Anastasia
   b. might have been Anastasia

4. More recently, some scientists believed that the bodies ....
   a. might not have been the czar's family
   b. had to have been the czar's family

DISCUSSION **BUILDER** • *Now discuss how believable a story is.*

Step 1. Group Work. Think of things you have done that might surprise your classmates. In groups of three, tell each other about one such experience.

> I studied to be an opera singer.

Step 2. Game: To tell the truth. In your group, choose one experience that all three of you will claim as your own. The rest of the class asks members of your group questions in order to determine which of you is telling the truth. Make your stories believable to your classmates.

> I studied to be an opera singer.

Some ideas for questions

How old were you when you did this?
Where exactly were you?
Were you alone or were other people with you?
What did you learn from the experience?
Your own question: ....

Finally, after all questions have been asked, the class takes a vote on who they think is telling the truth.

Step 3. Discussion. After each group plays the game, explain why you think some students' stories were more believable than others'.

> *"I thought your story was questionable because ...."*

> *"It was obvious that you were telling the truth because ...."*

4 *Evaluate the trustworthiness of news sources*

A **Reading Warm-up.** Look at the photos and headings in the magazine article. Are you familiar with either of these stories? What do you know about them?

B 🎧 **Reading.** Read the article. Why do you think so many people believed these stories?

Gerd Heidemann

Konrad Kujau

SPECIAL EDITION

The WORLD'S Greatest Hoaxes

Although they occurred fifty years apart, both of these spectacular hoaxes took the world by storm.

The Loch Ness Monster Story

Snapshot of the "Loch Ness Monster," published by the *Daily Mail*

It was quite a surprise when London's *Daily Mail* printed a photo in 1933 of a creature in Scotland's Loch Ness, the largest and deepest freshwater lake in the United Kingdom. People had been telling stories about such a creature for over a thousand years. But when a respected London surgeon, Colonel Robert Kenneth Wilson, took this photo, the stories suddenly seemed believable. He claimed that while driving by Loch Ness, he saw something strange in the water and quickly grabbed his camera. The photo he took was seen worldwide and began an increased public interest in the "Loch Ness Monster."

Sixty years later, in November 1993, Christian Spurling told a different story. His stepfather, filmmaker and actor Duke Wetherell, had been hired by the *Daily Mail* to look for evidence of the Loch Ness Monster. But instead, he asked his stepson, Spurling, to make a "monster" with his own hands—from a toy boat. His other son, Ian, took the photo. Then, in order to make the story believable, Wetherell asked the surgeon, Colonel Wilson, to say that he had taken the photo.

The story created so much publicity in 1933 that they decided not to admit the hoax. The true story remained a secret for over sixty years. In the meantime, those who believe there is a creature in the lake, continue to do so.

The "Hitler Diaries" Hoax

In 1983, the German magazine *Der Stern* announced that reporter Gerd Heidemann had made an incredible discovery: diaries written by Adolf Hitler. The magazine explained that the diaries had been found by farmers after a Nazi plane crashed in a field in April 1945. *Der Stern* paid almost 10 million marks to a Dr. Fischer, who claimed to have retrieved them.

The discovery caused a lot of excitement. Magazines and newspapers in London and New York rushed to print excerpts from the diaries, and scholars and researchers couldn't wait to get their hands on the material to learn more about the century's most infamous dictator. But some skeptics argued that the story couldn't be true—it was well-known that Hitler didn't like to take notes. Nonetheless, *Der Stern* insisted that the authenticity of the diaries was unquestionable.

However, when experts began to examine them, it became clear that the diaries were fake. It turned out that "Dr. Fischer" was actually Konrad Kujau, an art forger who had written the diaries himself, imitating Hitler's own handwriting. And both he and Heidemann had been putting the money from *Der Stern* into their own bank accounts. Both were sent to prison for fraud.

Interestingly, Kujau made a living selling copies of paintings by the world's greatest artists after he was released from prison.

Source: en.wikipedia.org

GLOSSARY	
admit =	tell the truth
claim =	say that something is true without proof
evidence =	information that proves that something is true
fake =	not real
a forger =	a person who makes things that aren't authentic, such as copies of famous paintings or money
fraud =	the crime of telling a lie to gain money
a hoax =	a story designed to make people believe something that isn't true
infamous =	well-known for having done something bad or morally evil
a skeptic =	a person who doesn't believe claims easily

C **Pair Work.** Discuss how best to complete each statement with names from the article.

The Loch Ness Monster Story

1. .... admitted that the Loch Ness Monster photo was a hoax.

2. The fake Loch Ness Monster was made by ....

3. .... didn't really take the photo of the Loch Ness Monster; the photo was actually taken by ....

4. The Loch Ness Monster hoax was created by ....

The "Hitler Diaries" Hoax

1. .... claimed to have discovered the Hitler Diaries.

2. *Der Stern*'s claim that .... had written the diary was questionable.

3. Konrad Kujau was claiming to be ....

4. The evidence showed that the Hitler Diaries were actually written by ....

5. *Der Stern* paid almost 10 million marks to .... and ...., not to Dr. Fischer.

D **Discussion.**

1. Why do you think the media get fooled by sensational hoaxes? Why do they seem to publish these stories so quickly?

2. Do you think hoaxes should be considered a crime, or are they harmless? Why?

DISCUSSION **BUILDER** • *Now evaluate the trustworthiness of news sources.*

Step 1. Pair Work. Complete the survey. Which of you do you think is more skeptical? Explain your answers.

Are you a skeptic?

	100%	90%	70%	50%	30%	10%	0%
What percentage of the news you read in the newspaper do you think is true?	○	○	○	○	○	○	○
What percentage of the news you hear on TV or radio do you think is true?	○	○	○	○	○	○	○
What percentage of what politicians say do you think is true?	○	○	○	○	○	○	○
What percentage of what you read on the Internet do you think is true?	○	○	○	○	○	○	○
What percentage of what advertisers say do you think is true?	○	○	○	○	○	○	○
What percentage of what your family says do you think is true?	○	○	○	○	○	○	○

Step 2. On your notepad, list media news sources from print, radio, TV, or the Internet that you trust and ones that you don't. Give reasons for your choices.

The news sources I trust the most	Some news sources I don't trust
Why?	Why not?

Step 3. Discussion. Why do you trust some news sources and not others? Do you and your classmates agree on any? How can you determine if the information you read or hear is true or not?

Writing: Write a news article

Avoiding sentence fragments

A sentence fragment is a group of words that does not express a complete thought.

Two common fragments are:

- **a dependent clause:** a group of words that contains a subject and a verb but begins with a subordinating conjunction, making it an incomplete thought.

    FRAGMENT: Because the banker admitted to fraud.

- **a phrase:** a group of words that does not contain a subject and a verb.

    FRAGMENT: With his help.
    FRAGMENT: At the end of the year.
    FRAGMENT: The man giving the speech.

To correct a sentence fragment, do one of the following:

- Attach the fragment to an independent clause to complete the thought.

    Because the banker admitted to fraud, **the bank was closed down.**

    We found the hospital with his help.

- Add a subject and / or a verb to make the fragment into a sentence.

    She graduated at the end of the year.
    The man giving the speech **needs a microphone.**

An independent clause:
- contains a subject and a verb
- expresses a complete thought

A complete sentence:
- starts with a capital letter
- ends with a period
- expresses a complete thought
- needs at least one independent clause

Subordinating conjunctions

after	since
as soon as	unless
because	until
before	when
even though	whenever
if	while

ERROR CORRECTION | Correct the three errors.

Benefit to Save Library

Last Wednesday, our town hosted a benefit concert. To help save the old building that used to be the library. Developers announced a plan to tear the building down. Two months ago. Because many people feel a connection to the library. The town decided to raise money to restore the building. The benefit concert was a success. Many local musicians performed, and we raised a lot of money.

Step 1. Prewriting. Generating ideas with information questions.

A news article usually answers information questions about an event. Think of a recent news event. This will be the topic of your article. On your notepad, write information questions about the topic to help generate ideas.

Topic:

Who?

What?

When?

Where?

Why?

How?

Step 2. Writing. On a separate sheet of paper, write an article about the event, answering your questions from Step 1. Try to include as much information as you can. Choose a title that reflects the main idea of your article.

Step 3. Self-Check.

☐ Did you write any sentence fragments? If so, correct them.
☐ Do you have a clear topic sentence?
☐ Is the article interesting? Could you add any more details?

SUMMIT WEBSITE
For Unit 9 online activities, visit the *Summit* Companion Website at
www.longman.com/summit.

A 🎧 **Listening Comprehension.** Listen to the conversations. Then listen to each conversation again and choose the statement that is closer in meaning to what each person said.

1. The woman said she thought ....
   a. it was possible Bill had overslept
   b. most likely Bill had overslept

2. The woman said she thought ....
   a. it was possible the wallet could be Gina's
   b. it was obvious the wallet was Gina's

3. The man said he thought ....
   a. the president may have been involved in the scandal
   b. the president had clearly been involved in the scandal

4. The man said he thought ....
   a. the story could possibly be a hoax
   b. the story couldn't possibly be true

B Change each sentence from direct to indirect speech.

1. She said, "The job will be completed by Monday."

   ....

2. He told me, "Your parents should take the early flight."

   ....

3. My boss said, "Rita may be interested in visiting the art museum."

   ....

4. The school director told us, "Your children must come to class on time."

   ....

5. The clerk said to him, "Your package can be picked up anytime before 5:00 P.M."

   ....

6. The agent told them, "Your passports have to be renewed by tomorrow."

   ....

C On a separate sheet of paper, write your *own* response to each question, using varying degrees of certainty. Explain your theory.

I suppose it's possible, but I really don't believe it . . .

1. Do you think Bigfoot is real?

2. We know that the photograph of the Loch Ness Monster was a hoax, but do you think the Loch Ness Monster exists?

3. Do you believe there's something mysterious about the Bermuda Triangle that causes ships to disappear?

4. Do you think the damage to the forests in Tunguska was caused by a meteorite?

UNIT 10

Your Free Time

UNIT GOALS

1 Explain the benefits of leisure activities
2 Describe hobbies and other interests
3 Compare your use of leisure time
4 Discuss the risk-taking personality

A **Topic Preview.** Read about these technological advances. Do you know of any other inventions that didn't achieve their promises?

Does technology always live up to its promises?

The promise
Cars were supposed to make it easy to get away from it all.

The reality
Drivers today spend an average of 101 minutes a day driving. And they spend over 40 hours a year stuck in traffic.

The promise
Television was supposed to bring families closer for quality time together.

The reality
Families spend an average of 170 minutes a day watching TV—a lot more time than they spend talking to each other.

The promise
New household appliances were supposed to increase free time and cut back on time spent doing chores.

The reality
Despite increased spending on "laborsaving" devices, people still spend an average of 23.5 hours a week on housework—the same as people living at the beginning of the 20th century.

Information based on U.S. and Canadian government statistics

B **Discussion.**

1. In your opinion, what technological advances *do* save us time?
2. With all the laborsaving and timesaving inventions available to us today, why is it that everybody complains about not having enough free time?

C 🎧 **Sound Bites.** Read and listen to a conversation between two close friends at the office.

ED: I can't take it anymore. This job is really getting to me.

KIM: Hey, sounds like you could use a break.

ED: Are you kidding? I'm up to my ears in paperwork.

KIM: When was the last time you took some time off?

ED: Come to think of it, it's been over a year. I was supposed to take off a few weeks in January, but it just got too busy around here.

KIM: Then it sounds like a little R and R* would do you some good.

ED: You're right. And anyway, I can always bring my laptop along and catch up on my work.

KIM: Listen, leave the laptop at home! You need to just take it easy for a while.

* R and R = rest and relaxation

D **In Other Words.** Read the conversation again. With a partner, explain the meaning of the following statements.

1. "This job is really getting to me."

2. "Are you kidding?"

3. "I'm up to my ears in paperwork."

4. "A little R and R would do you some good."

5. "I can catch up on my work."

6. "You need to just take it easy."

STARTING **POINT**

How do you usually spend your free time? Check all that apply.

- ☐ I hang out with other people.
- ☐ I spend my time alone.
- ☐ I take it easy.
- ☐ I find something exciting to do.
- ☐ I catch up on the chores I never have time for.
- ☐ I catch up on work.
- ☐ I use my time to learn something new.
- ☐ I sit around and worry about what I need to do.
- ☐ Other: ....

Pair Work. Compare how you spend your free time. How similar are you and your partner?

1 Explain the benefits of leisure activities

A ⌒ CONVERSATION **SNAPSHOT**

A: I've taken up Go recently. Do you play?

B: No. I've never even heard of it. What's Go?

A: It's a great Japanese game. Kind of like chess.

B: I hate to say this, but I find chess a little boring.

A: Well, even so, you should give it a try. I think it's intellectually stimulating. I'm sure you'd like it.

⌒ **Rhythm and intonation practice**

the board game Go (Japan)

B ⌒ Word Skills. Using collocations for leisure activities. Add your own game, fitness activity, hobby, or handicraft.

"I **play chess**."
"I **play video games**."

Do you **play** any interesting **games**?

Your own game:
....

"I **play Ping-Pong**."

"I **do karate**."
"I **do aerobics**."

Do you **do** any **fitness activities**?

Your own fitness activity:
....

"I **do yoga**."

"I **do embroidery**."
"I **do wood carving**."

Do you **do** any **handicrafts**?

Your own handicraft:
....

"I **crochet**."

"I **raise rabbits**."
"I **restore antiques**."

Do you **have** any **hobbies**?

Your own hobby:
....

"I **collect coins**."

C Discussion. Which, if any, leisure activities do you do? Which would you like to take up someday? Which activities are the most popular in your class?

D **Word Skills. Modifying with adverbs.** Use an adverb to modify a verb or an adjective. Many adverbs are formed by adding -*ly* to an adjective.

Karate challenges you **physically**. You have to work your body really hard if you want to be good at it. [modifies verb]

I find chess **intellectually** stimulating. You have to use your head to play it well. [modifies adjective]

Adjectives	Adverbs
creative	→ **creatively**
emotional	→ **emotionally**
financial	→ **financially**
intellectual	→ **intellectually**
physical	→ **physically**
social	→ **socially**
spiritual	→ **spiritually**

Grammar Booster

PAGE G16
for more...

E Complete the statements with an appropriate adverb. Compare your choices with a partner.

1. Building one-of-a-kind furniture is what makes woodworking so .... satisfying.

2. While it doesn't feature the punching and kicking found in karate or kung fu, a serious yoga workout can be as .... difficult as any martial art.

3. Even though there are computer programs that can defeat the greatest chess players, there has never been a program "smart" enough to win the .... challenging game of Go.

4. They say raising tropical fish can really set you back .... They're very expensive.

F **Pair Work.** Recommend a leisure activity for each of the people below. Explain why you made that choice.

I've just opened up my own graphic design business. I'm also a full-time mom. Balancing work and family is really challenging. When I do get some free time, I need to do something creative.

Suzy Tanaka

"I think Suzy should take up some kind of handicraft. She might find it relaxing, and it might stimulate her creatively."

I'm a businessperson, and my job is very demanding. Sometimes the stress really gets to me. I have to travel a lot for work—I'm on the go from morning to night. I often get headaches and backaches from all the tension. I really need to get some R and R into my life.

Solange Teixeira

Being a computer programmer, I have to sit at a desk all day long. I work long hours, and by the time I get home at night, I'm pretty exhausted. The only free time I have is on the weekends. But even then, I can't always let go of the job. I've got to find a way to take my mind off of work.

Lionel Espinoza

CONVERSATION **STARTER** • *Now explain the benefits of leisure activities.*

Pair Work. Discuss and list leisure activities you think fit in each category.

physically challenging	emotionally satisfying	intellectually stimulating	just plain fun!

Talk to your partner about a leisure activity you have taken up or that you would like to try. Explain why you like it. Use the Conversation Snapshot on page 112 as a guide. Start like this: "I've taken up .... recently."

2 Describe hobbies and other interests

A 🎧 GRAMMAR **SNAPSHOT.** Read the message-board posts and notice the use of noun modifiers.

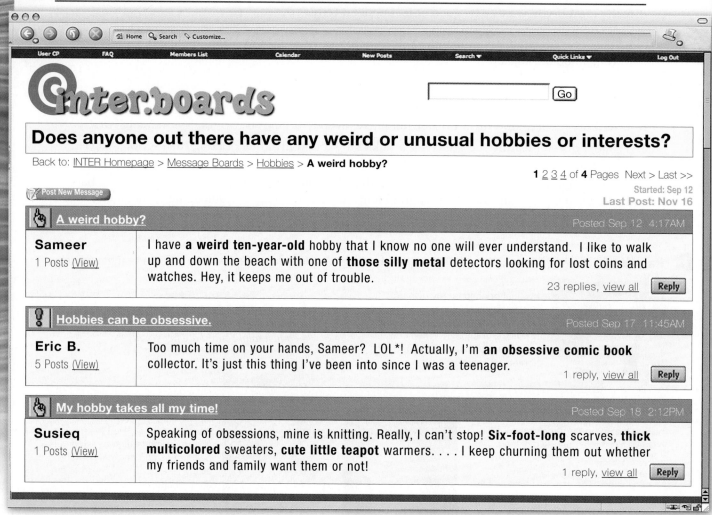

*LOL = laughing out loud

B **Grammar.** Order of modifiers

When a noun is modified by more than one word, modifiers usually appear in the following order.

❶ **determiners:** a, an, the, this, my, Judy's
❷ **ordinals:** first, one thousandth
❸ **quantifiers:** one, a few, some, many
❹ **adjectives** (in the following order):
   size: small, huge, tall, wide
   an opinion or quality: beautiful, clear, weird, obsessive
   age or temperature: young, middle-aged, antique, freezing
   shape: round, triangular
   color: black, greenish
   origin: British, handmade
   material: glass, silk, metal
❺ **nouns:** student, childhood, book, teapot

my first few beautiful antique Czech crystal sugar bowls
  ❶ ❷ ❸   ❹   ❺

BE CAREFUL! When the modifier is a noun, never use a plural form.
  a delicious **vegetable** soup
  NOT a delicious ~~vegetables~~ soup

BE CAREFUL! Hyphenate compound modifiers when they precede the noun. Don't use a plural form.
  a **two-year-old** house
  NOT a two-~~years~~-old house
  BUT The house is two years old.

Grammar Booster
PAGE G16
for more...

C On a separate sheet of paper, rewrite each sentence, correcting the order of the noun modifiers.

1. Are you going to wear that green ugly cotton shirt?

2. That was the most interesting French old film I've ever seen.

3. I gave her a wooden beautiful round box that I picked up during my trip.

4. She bought an Italian hundred-year-old expensive violin.

5. Isn't this the third mystery historical novel you've read this month?

6. He bought her a silk white gorgeous handkerchief.

D Complete the sentences with compound modifiers, using the descriptions in parentheses.

1. She bought a new .... bike.
   (It has ten speeds.)

2. They offer a .... introductory class at the new yoga school.
   (It runs for three months.)

3. We gave her a small .... pillow.
   (It was embroidered by hand.)

4. The company sent him a .... letter.
   (It was filled with praise.)

5. The government announced a .... plan for protecting
   (It has five points.)
   the environment.

GRAMMAR **EXCHANGE** • *Now describe hobbies and other interests.*

Think of some things you and people you know like to do or make. On your notepad, write sentences about these hobbies or interests, using at least three noun modifiers to describe each.

> I've been collecting *beautiful antique handmade paper* dolls for years.
> My sister has always liked to watch *old black-and-white Hollywood* movies.

Group Work. Walk around the classroom and interview your classmates about the hobbies and interests they wrote about on their notepads. Then tell your class about the most interesting hobbies or interests you heard about, using noun modifiers.

3 *Compare your use of leisure time*

A **Reading Warm-up.** Are you satisfied with the amount of leisure time you have in your life?

B 🎧 **Reading.** Read the article. What's the author's main point about technology today?

IS TECHNOLOGY KILLING LEISURE TIME?

by Jon Katz

New surveys suggest that the technological tools we use to make our lives easier are killing our leisure time. We are working longer hours, taking fewer and shorter vacations (and when we do go away, we take our cell phones, PDAs, and laptops along). And we are more stressed than ever as increased use of e-mail, voice mail, cell phones, and the Internet are destroying any idea of privacy and leisure.

Since the Industrial Revolution, people have assumed that new laborsaving devices would free them from the burdens of the workplace and give them more time to grow intellectually, creatively, and socially— exploring the arts, keeping up with current events, spending more time with friends and family, and even just "goofing off."

But here we are at the start of the 21st century, enjoying one of the greatest technological boom times in human history, and nothing could be further from the truth. The very tools that were supposed to liberate us have bound us to our work and study in ways that were inconceivable just a few years ago. It would seem that technology almost never does what we expect.

In "the old days," the lines between work and leisure time were markedly clearer. People left their offices at a predictable time, were often completely disconnected from and out of touch with their jobs as they traveled to and from work, and were off-duty once they were home. That's no longer true. In today's highly competitive job market, employers demand increased productivity, expecting workers to put in longer hours and to keep in touch almost constantly via fax, cell phones, e-mail, or other communications devices. As a result, employees feel the need to check in on what's going on at the office, even on days off. They feel pressured to work after hours just to catch up on everything they have to do. Workers work harder and longer, change their work tasks more frequently, and have more and more reasons to worry about job security.

Bosses, colleagues, and family members—lovers, friends, and spouses too—expect instant responses to voice mail and e-mail messages. Even college students have become bound to their desks by an environment in which faculty, friends, and other members of the college community increasingly do their work online. Studies of time spent on instant messaging services would probably show staggering use.

This isn't what technology was supposed to be doing for us. New technologies, from genetic research to the Internet, offer all sorts of benefits and opportunities. But when new tools make life more difficult and stressful rather than easier and more meaningful—and we are, as a society, barely conscious of it—then something has gone seriously awry, both with our expectations for technology and our understanding of how it should benefit us.

Reprinted from slashdot.org; written by Jon Katz

C Discussion.

1. The author states that advances in technology such as e-mail, voice mail, cell phones, and the Internet are "destroying any idea of privacy and leisure." How do you think each of these technologies do that in his view? Give specific examples.

2. The author states that "technology almost never does what we expect." What expectations do people have each time a new technology appears? Give examples with specific technologies.

3. Do you agree with the author's point of view in the article? Why or why not?

DISCUSSION **BUILDER** • *Now compare your use of leisure time.*

Step 1. Complete the survey. Then circle the activities you truly consider to be "leisure activities."

✔ Check how frequently you do each of the following activities.

	Very often	Frequently	Sometimes	Rarely	Never
running errands	○	○	○	○	○
doing housework	○	○	○	○	○
surfing the Web	○	○	○	○	○
catching up on personal e-mail	○	○	○	○	○
keeping in touch with friends by telephone	○	○	○	○	○
spending time with family	○	○	○	○	○
attending cultural events	○	○	○	○	○
working on a hobby or interest	○	○	○	○	○
playing games (video, board games, sports)	○	○	○	○	○
reading for pleasure	○	○	○	○	○
listening to music	○	○	○	○	○
watching TV	○	○	○	○	○
exercising	○	○	○	○	○
taking naps	○	○	○	○	○
eating out	○	○	○	○	○
other:	○	○	○	○	○

Source: www.questionpro.com

Step 2. Pair Work. Compare how you spend your time. Which activities do you wish you spent more time on? Are there any you think you spend too much time on?

Step 3. Discussion. In what ways does technology add to or interfere with your leisure time? What can you do to keep work or study balanced with leisure time in your life?

"E-mail keeps me in touch with more of my friends. I don't think it interferes with my leisure time at all."

4 Discuss the risk-taking personality

Do people who ride roller coasters have a "big T" or "small t" personality?

A 🎧 **Listening Comprehension.** Listen to the interview with a psychologist. Then listen again and write a description for each of the two personality types the psychologist describes.

What is a "big T" personality?	What is a "small t" personality?

B **Discussion.** Where do you fit on the risk-taking continuum? Do you have a "big T" or a "small t" personality? Give examples to support your opinion.

← RISK-TAKER ——————————— RISK-AVOIDER →

C 🎧 **Vocabulary. Ways to express fear and fearlessness.** Listen and practice.

Pronunciation Booster
PAGE P10
Vowel sounds

I can't wait to go hang gliding.

I wouldn't dare go hang gliding.

Skydiving **doesn't scare me a bit.**

Skydiving **scares the life out of me.**

There's nothing like surfing.

There's not a chance I would go surfing.

I can't get enough of white-water rafting.

You wouldn't catch me white-water rafting.

Bungee jumping is no sweat.

You'd have to be out of your mind to go bungee jumping.

118 UNIT 10

LISTENING

D **Pair Work.** Use the expressions from the vocabulary to discuss which extreme sports you would or would not be willing to do.

> "Rock climbing scares the life out of me."

waterfall jumping

surfing

rock climbing

mountain biking

extreme skiing

skydiving

DISCUSSION **BUILDER** • *Now discuss the risk-taking personality.*

Step 1. Pair Work. What's the riskiest thing your partner has ever done? Interview him or her and take notes on your notepad. Where would *you* place your partner on the risk-taking continuum?

What?	Other details:
Where?	
When?	
How?	

Step 2. Group Work. In small groups, compare your partners' experiences. Then decide who is the most fearless.

Step 3. Discussion.

1. In your opinion, why does one person develop into a risk-taker and another into a risk-avoider?
2. Do you think risk-taking is a healthy type of behavior? Where do you think the best place to be on the risk-taking continuum is? Why?

Writing: Comment on another's point of view

Expressing and supporting your opinion

When you write to critique or comment on another's spoken or written ideas, present your reasons logically, using connecting words to give reasons and to sequence your ideas.

Giving reasons

I disagree **because** I think people actually have lots of free time today.

This is why I think the author is wrong.

We definitely have more free time **since** we are able to work from home.

On account of people using laptops, they get work done faster.

Sequencing ideas

First of all, I agree with Jon Katz's main point.

I **also** think he makes a good point about modern technology.

In addition, I think he's right about technology in the workplace.

Finally, we need to decide what we want technology to do for us.

WRITING MODEL

I disagree with almost all of Jon Katz's ideas in his article "Is Technology Killing Leisure Time?" **since** most new inventions actually help us increase the time we have for leisure activities. **First of all,** when Katz says, "Technology almost never does what we expect," he is ignoring the popularity of most new technologies. If a technology did not achieve its promise, it would not be so popular. **In addition,** I

Step 1. Prewriting. Developing arguments.

Read the article "Is Technology Killing Leisure Time?" on page 116 and underline sentences that you agree with or do not agree with. On a separate sheet of paper, do the following:

- paraphrase each sentence you underlined
- provide the reasons why you agree or disagree

Quoting the author

You can write short statements in direct speech using quotes, as shown in the Writing Model. Paraphrase longer statements in indirect speech.

The author says that technology almost never does what we expect. I disagree because it isn't true for most new inventions. The popularity of most new technologies proves that people are happy with them.

Step 2. Writing. On a separate sheet of paper, write a critique of the article. State your own opinion at the beginning. Use the sentences you underlined and the comments you wrote to support your opinion.

Step 3. Self-Check.

- ☐ Is your opinion clearly stated?
- ☐ Did you use connecting words to support your reasons and sequence your ideas?
- ☐ Did you use quotation marks when using the author's own words?
- ☐ Did you paraphrase the author's words when you didn't use direct speech?

SUMMIT WEBSITE
For Unit 10 online activities, visit the *Summit* Companion Website at www.longman.com/summit.

A 🎧 **Listening Comprehension.** Listen to the conversations about free time. Infer the kind of leisure activity the people are discussing.

1. ☐ a game   ☐ a fitness activity   ☐ a hobby   ☐ a handicraft
2. ☐ a game   ☐ a fitness activity   ☐ a hobby   ☐ a handicraft
3. ☐ a game   ☐ a fitness activity   ☐ a hobby   ☐ a handicraft
4. ☐ a game   ☐ a fitness activity   ☐ a hobby   ☐ a handicraft

B Categorize the leisure activities in the box. Use a dictionary for words you don't know. Add other activities.

hobbies	games	handicrafts	fitness activities

collecting stamps   lifting weights
making jewelry   sewing
playing checkers   doing puzzles
doing tae kwon do   knitting
playing cards   restoring old cars
growing roses   raising iguanas

C Use the words in the box to modify the nouns. Use at least three modifiers for each noun.

a / an	this / that	his / her	new	intelligent	English
some	many	green	stylish	black	handmade
adorable	destructive	sincere	clever	antique	South American
flashy	young	small	cotton	friendly	law

1. .... sweater
2. .... parrot
3. .... student
4. .... teacup

D Complete the statements in your *own* way.

1. .... scares the life out of me.
2. You'd have to be out of your mind to ....
3. You wouldn't catch me ....
4. .... doesn't scare me a bit.
5. I can't wait to ....
6. There's nothing like ....

Pronunciation table

These are the pronunciation symbols used in *Summit 1*.

Vowels

Symbol	Key Word	Symbol	Key Word
i	beat, feed	ə	banana, among
ɪ	bit, did	ɚ	shirt, murder
eɪ	date, paid	aɪ	bite, cry, buy, eye
ɛ	bet, bed	aʊ	about, how
æ	bat, bad	ɔɪ	voice, boy
ɑ	box, odd, father	ɪr	beer
ɔ	bought, dog	ɛr	bare
oʊ	boat, road	ɑr	bar
ʊ	book, good	ɔr	door
u	boot, food, student	ʊr	tour
ʌ	but, mud, mother		

Consonants

Symbol	Key Word	Symbol	Key Word
p	pack, happy	z	zip, please, goes
b	back, rubber	ʃ	ship, machine, station, special, discussion
t	tie		
d	die		
k	came, key, quick	ʒ	measure, vision
g	game, guest	h	hot, who
tʃ	church, nature, watch	m	men, some
		n	sun, know, pneumonia
dʒ	judge, general, major	ŋ	sung, ringing
f	fan, photograph	w	wet, white
v	van	l	light, long
θ	thing, breath	r	right, wrong
ð	then, breathe	y	yes, use, music
s	sip, city, psychology	ṭ	butter, bottle
		t˺	button

Irregular verbs

base form	simple past	past participle
be	was / were	been
beat	beat	beaten
become	became	become
begin	began	begun
bend	bent	bent
bet	bet	bet
bite	bit	bitten
bleed	bled	bled
blow	blew	blown
break	broke	broken
breed	bred	bred
bring	brought	brought
build	built	built
burn	burned / burnt	burned / burnt
burst	burst	burst
buy	bought	bought
catch	caught	caught
choose	chose	chosen
come	came	come
cost	cost	cost
creep	crept	crept
cut	cut	cut
deal	dealt	dealt
dig	dug	dug
do	did	done
draw	drew	drawn
dream	dreamed / dreamt	dreamed / dreamt
drink	drank	drunk
drive	drove	driven
eat	ate	eaten
fall	fell	fallen
feed	fed	fed
feel	felt	felt
fight	fought	fought
find	found	found
fit	fit	fit
fly	flew	flown
forbid	forbade	forbidden

base form	simple past	past participle
forget	forgot	forgotten
forgive	forgave	forgiven
freeze	froze	frozen
get	got	gotten
give	gave	given
go	went	gone
grow	grew	grown
hang	hung	hung
have	had	had
hear	heard	heard
hide	hid	hidden
hit	hit	hit
hold	held	held
hurt	hurt	hurt
keep	kept	kept
know	knew	known
lay	laid	laid
lead	led	led
leap	leaped / leapt	leaped / leapt
learn	learned / learnt	learned / learnt
leave	left	left
lend	lent	lent
let	let	let
lie	lay	lain
light	lit	lit
lose	lost	lost
make	made	made
mean	meant	meant
meet	met	met
mistake	mistook	mistaken
pay	paid	paid
put	put	put
quit	quit	quit
read /rid/	read /rɛd/	read /rɛd/
ride	rode	ridden
ring	rang	rung
rise	rose	risen
run	ran	run

base form	simple past	past participle	base form	simple past	past participle
say	said	said	spring	sprang / sprung	sprang / sprung
see	saw	seen	stand	stood	stood
sell	sold	sold	steal	stole	stolen
send	sent	sent	stick	stuck	stuck
set	set	set	sting	stung	stung
shake	shook	shaken	stink	stank / stunk	stunk
shed	shed	shed	strike	struck	struck / stricken
shine	shone	shone	string	strung	strung
shoot	shot	shot	swear	swore	sworn
show	showed	shown	sweep	swept	swept
shrink	shrank	shrunk	swim	swam	swum
shut	shut	shut	swing	swung	swung
sing	sang	sung	take	took	taken
sink	sank	sunk	teach	taught	taught
sit	sat	sat	tear	tore	torn
sleep	slept	slept	tell	told	told
slide	slid	slid	think	thought	thought
smell	smelled / smelt	smelled / smelt	throw	threw	thrown
speak	spoke	spoken	understand	understood	understood
speed	sped / speeded	sped / speeded	upset	upset	upset
spell	spelled / spelt	spelled / spelt	wake	woke / waked	woken / waked
spend	spent	spent	wear	wore	worn
spill	spilled / spilt	spilled / spilt	weave	wove	woven
spin	spun	spun	weep	wept	wept
spit	spit / spat	spit / spat	win	won	won
spoil	spoiled / spoilt	spoiled / spoilt	wind	wound	wound
spread	spread	spread	write	wrote	written

Stative verbs

amaze	desire	hear	need	seem
appear*	dislike	imagine	owe	smell*
appreciate	doubt	include*	own	sound
astonish	envy	know	please	suppose
be*	equal	like	possess	surprise
believe	exist	look like	prefer	taste*
belong	fear	look*	realize	think*
care	feel*	love	recognize	understand
consist of	forget	matter	remember*	want *
contain	hate	mean	resemble	weigh*
cost	have*	mind	see*	

*These verbs also have action meanings. Example: I see a tree. (non-action) I'm seeing her tomorrow. (action)

Verbs that can be followed by a gerund

admit	dislike	miss	resist
appreciate	don't mind	postpone	risk
avoid	enjoy	practice	suggest
can't help	finish	quit	tolerate
complete	keep (as in *continue*)	recall	understand
consider	mention	recommend	
discuss	mind (as in *object to*)	resent	

Expressions that can be followed by a gerund

be excited about	be opposed to	believe in	blame [someone or something] for
be worried about	be used to	participate in	forgive [someone or something] for
be responsible for	complain about	succeed in	thank [someone or something] for
be interested in	dream about / of	take advantage of	keep [someone or something] from
be accused of	talk about / of	take care of	prevent [someone or something] from
be capable of	think about / of	insist on	stop [someone or something] from
be tired of	apologize for	look forward to	
be accustomed to	make an excuse for		
be committed to	have a reason for		

Verbs that can be followed directly by an infinitive

afford	deserve	offer	swear
agree	expect	plan	threaten
appear	fail	prepare	volunteer
arrange	hesitate	pretend	wait
ask	hope	promise	want
care	intend	refuse	wish
claim	learn	regret	would like
decide	mean	seem	
demand	need	struggle	

Verbs that must be followed by an object before an infinitive

advise	encourage	invite	require
allow	expect	need	teach
ask	forbid	order	tell
beg	force	permit	urge
cause	help	persuade	want
challenge	hire	promise	warn
convince	instruct	remind	would like

Adjectives that can be followed by an infinitive

anxious	depressed	lucky	relieved
ashamed	disappointed	pleased	sad
certain	fortunate	prepared	sorry
content	glad	proud	upset
delighted	happy	ready	

Verbs that can be followed by a gerund or an infinitive

with a change in meaning

forget (+ gerund)	=	forget something that happened
(+ infinitive)	=	forget something that needs to be done
regret (+ gerund)	=	regret a past action
(+ infinitive)	=	regret having to inform someone about an action
remember (+ gerund)	=	remember something that happened
(+ infinitive)	=	remember something that needs to be done
stop (+ gerund)	=	stop a continuous action
(+ infinitive)	=	stop in order to do something

without a change in meaning

begin	love
can't stand	prefer
continue	start
hate	try
like	

Participial adjectives

alarming	–	alarmed	disturbing	–	disturbed	paralyzing	–	paralyzed
amazing	–	amazed	embarrassing	–	embarrassed	pleasing	–	pleased
amusing	–	amused	entertaining	–	entertained	relaxing	–	relaxed
annoying	–	annoyed	exciting	–	excited	satisfying	–	satisfied
astonishing	–	astonished	exhausting	–	exhausted	shocking	–	shocked
boring	–	bored	fascinating	–	fascinated	soothing	–	soothed
comforting	–	comforted	frightening	–	frightened	startling	–	startled
confusing	–	confused	horrifying	–	horrified	stimulating	–	stimulated
depressing	–	depressed	inspiring	–	inspired	surprising	–	surprised
disappointing	–	disappointed	interesting	–	interested	terrifying	–	terrified
disgusting	–	disgusted	irritating	–	irritated	tiring	–	tired
distressing	–	distressed	moving	–	moved	touching	–	touched

Grammar Booster

The *Grammar Booster* is optional. It provides more explanation and practice as well as additional grammar concepts.

Unit 1

Gerunds and infinitives: summary

Gerunds

A gerund functions as a noun. A gerund or gerund phrase can be the subject of a sentence, a direct or indirect object, a subject complement, or the object of a preposition.

Living a balanced life is about integrating all parts of it. [subject]
I love spending time with my family. [direct object]
The best part of life is learning new things. [subject complement]
Here are some tips for getting a healthy perspective on life. [object of a preposition]

Infinitives

An infinitive also functions as a noun. An infinitive or infinitive phrase can be the subject of a sentence, but infinitives as subjects are often considered awkward. It is more common to use an impersonal It as the subject.

To be honest isn't always easy. [subject]
OR It isn't always easy to be honest.

An infinitive or infinitive phrase can be a direct object or a subject complement.

I want to feel less stressed. [direct object]
My favorite thing is to spend time with friends. [subject complement]

An infinitive or infinitive phrase can express a purpose.

Make time to relax.
We stopped to buy some gas.

REMEMBER

Some verbs can only be followed by a gerund.
I suggest asking her if she can make it.
We finished writing the report.
He recommends not waiting till the last minute.

Some verbs can only be followed by an infinitive.
You should expect to be there by early afternoon.
I hope to complete the course.
Learn not to live in the past.

Some verbs can be followed by a gerund or an infinitive with no change in meaning.
He likes listening to jazz.
He likes to listen to jazz.

Some verbs require an object before an infinitive.
He reminded me to call my mother.
I persuaded them not to sell their house.
The school permitted her to skip the first level.

Some adjectives can be followed by an infinitive.
He was surprised to get the promotion.
I was disappointed to hear the news.

For a complete list of verbs, adjectives, and expressions followed by gerunds and infinitives, see page A3 in the Appendices.

A Complete each sentence with a gerund or infinitive form of the verb. Refer to page A3 in the Appendices if necessary.

1. We were delighted .... out that we had won the contest.
   (find)

2. Be sure to thank your father for .... me get that interview.
   (help)

3. She goes to the gym five times a week .... in shape.
   (stay)

4. Don't be surprised if he refuses .... with them.
   (cooperate)

5. .... other people for help is sometimes hard to do.
   (ask)

6. They definitely won't permit you .... that on board.
   (carry)

B On a separate sheet of paper, rewrite the following sentences, using an impersonal It as the subject of the sentence.

1. To pass the examination is not the easiest thing in the world.

2. To speak English fluently is my greatest wish.

3. To live in an English-speaking country might be an exciting experience.

4. To know when to use an infinitive and when to use a gerund is pretty confusing.

Grammar for Writing: parallelism with gerunds and infinitives

A common error in formal written English is mixing gerunds and infinitives when listing items in a series. A list of items should either be all gerunds or all infinitives.

When I take time off from work, I prefer **relaxing** at home, **spending** time with my family, and **getting** things done around the house.

NOT I prefer relaxing at home, spending time with my family, and ~~to get~~ things done around the house.

I can't stand **getting up** late and **missing** the bus.

NOT I can't stand getting up late and ~~to miss~~ the bus.

In a series, either use <u>to</u> with all the infinitives or only with the first one.

When I take time off from work, I prefer **to relax** at home, **spend** time with my family, and **get** things done around the house.

NOT When I take time off from work, I prefer to relax at home, spend time with my family, and ~~to get~~ things done around the house.

C On a separate sheet of paper, correct the errors in parallelism in the following sentences.

1. After she arrived in London, she began to write long letters home and calling her parents at all hours of the night.

2. There are two things I really can't stand doing: speaking in front of large audiences and chat with people I don't know at parties.

3. Right before midnight, everyone began to sing, dance, and to welcome in the new year.

4. There's no question I prefer using all my vacation time and take a long vacation.

D Complete the following sentences, using appropriate gerund or infinitive forms. Refer to page A3 in the Appendices if necessary.

1. I would suggest .... out the form immediately and .... a copy for
   _(fill) _(make)
   your records.

2. Did you remember .... off the stove, ... the windows, and
   _(turn) _(close)
   .... the door before you left?
   _(lock)

3. It's obvious from her e-mails that she really loves .... the culture, ...
   _(experience) _(meet)
   new people, and just .... there.
   _(be)

4. I don't think they permit .... photographs or .... a recorder.
   _(take) _(use)

5. I really wouldn't mind .... them out to dinner or .... them
   _(take) _(show)
   around if you'd like me to.

6. He promised .... the report home, ... it carefully, and ....
   _(take) _(read) _(respond)
   to any questions by the next day.

Unit 2

Finished and unfinished actions: summary

Finished actions

Use the simple past tense or the past of <u>be</u> for an action finished at a specified time in the past.
They **watched** that DVD yesterday.

Use the present perfect for an action finished at an unspecified time in the past.
They**'ve watched** that DVD three times.

Use the past perfect for an action that was finished before another action in the past.
When I arrived, they **had** already **watched** the DVD.

NOTE: Although the continuous aspect is used for actions in progress, the present perfect continuous is sometimes used for very recently completed actions, especially to emphasize duration.
They**'ve been watching** that DVD all afternoon, but they're done now.

Unfinished actions

Use the present perfect OR the present perfect continuous for unfinished actions that began in the past and may continue into the future. Use the present perfect continuous to further emphasize that the action is continuous.
She**'s listened** to Ray Charles for years. [And she may continue.]
OR She**'s been listening** to Ray Charles for years. [And she may continue.]

A Complete the article, using the simple past tense, the past of <u>be</u>, or the present perfect.

World Music is not really a true genre of music—it is a combination of musical genres from around the

world. For a number of years, recording companies .... the term to describe the music of artists who
(1. use)

they feel could appeal to new audiences across cultures. The concept of World Music .... first created
(2. be)

after U.S. singer / songwriter Paul Simon .... his hugely successful *Graceland* album in 1986. At that
(3. record)

time, he .... South Africa's male choir Ladysmith Black Mambazo and rock group Savuka to accompany
(4. invite)

him on the recording. Both groups later .... with him around the world. This exciting collaboration
(5. tour)

immediately .... to European and North American audiences, who were attracted to this different sound.
(6. appeal)

Since that time, as more artists .... to reach new audiences, there .... an increased amount
(7. try)   (8. be)

of "crossover"—that is, musicians influencing each other across cultures. Enthusiasm for music from other cultures

.... steadily. Artists such as Angélique Kidjo and Carlos Vives, who were well-known within specific
(9. rise)

regions such as Africa or Latin America, ... international stars, and mainstream music ....
(10. become)   (11. incorporate)

many of the features of these artists.

B Read each statement. Then decide which description is closer in meaning.

1. By the time I heard about it, the concert had sold out.
   a. First I heard about the concert. Then it sold out.
   b. First the concert sold out. Then I heard about it.

2. After he'd won the award, he got a big recording contract.
   a. First he got the recording contract. Then he won the award.
   b. First he won the award. Then he got the recording contract.

3. We wanted to go to his performance because we'd heard his new CD.
   a. First we heard his CD. Then we wanted to go to his performance.
   b. First we wanted to go to his performance. Then we heard his CD.

4. He'd played at a lot of different halls before he performed at Carnegie Hall.
   a. First he performed at Carnegie Hall. Then he played at a lot of different halls.
   b. First he played at a lot of different halls. Then he performed at Carnegie Hall.

The past perfect continuous

Use the past perfect continuous for a continuous action that occurred and finished before an earlier time or event.

By 1998, he **had been studying** French for about five years.

When the test began, the students **had been waiting** for over an hour.

NOTE: This structure tends to occur more in formal writing than in speaking.

C Use the present perfect continuous or the past perfect continuous to complete each statement.

1. Stella is such a big fan of Bob Marley that she .... nothing but his recordings for years.
   (collect)

2. Jill Morsberger .... at clubs for ten years before Greenwood Entertainment invited her
   (perform)
   to sign a recording contract.

3. Jeff .... at the airport for his girlfriend when he saw the lead singer for U2.
   (wait)

4. She must be extremely popular. The audience .... in line to buy tickets for over two
   (stand)
   hours.

5. The lead guitarist for the band .... the new songs for weeks. That's why they sound
   (rehearse)
   so good tonight.

6. Shakira .... songs only in Spanish before she decided to branch out and try recording
   (record)
   songs in English for the U.S. market.

Grammar for Writing: noun clauses as adjective and noun complements

Noun clauses as subjects are awkward and generally avoided.
Two ways to rewrite such sentences follow.

Use a noun clause as an adjective complement.

AVOIDED **That Frankel is quite critical of modern art is obvious.**
PREFERRED **It is obvious (that) Frankel is quite critical of modern art.**

Use a noun clause as a noun complement.

AVOIDED **That her job was so difficult was why she quit.**
PREFERRED **The fact that her job was so difficult was why she quit.**

Impersonal expressions that introduce noun clauses
It is **important** (that)
It appears **obvious** (that)
It seems **clear** (that)
It becomes **essential** (that)
It is **possible** (that)
It looks **likely** (that)

Noun phrases that can precede a noun clause

the announcement that	the news that
the argument that	the possibility that
the belief that	the proposal that
the chance that	the reason that
the claim that	the recommendation that
the demand that	the report that
the fact that	the suggestion that
the idea that	

The reason that she refuses to appear in films is a mystery to everyone.
The argument that classical music is dead makes no sense.
The news that the new CEO is retiring surprised a lot of people.

D On a separate sheet of paper, rewrite each sentence, using the impersonal <u>It</u>.

1. That developing countries address the problems caused by global warming is extremely important.
2. That the president plans on resigning appears obvious to everyone.
3. That not providing disaster relief will only worsen the situation seems quite clear.
4. That a cure for cancer will be discovered in the next twenty years is certainly possible.
5. That the governments of Argentina and Chile will reach an agreement looks very likely.
6. That Max Bianchi won't be participating in the Olympics next year is not important.

E Read each quote from a radio news program. Then, on a separate sheet of paper, complete each statement, using the noun clause as a noun complement.

Example: "Volkswagen announced that they would unveil a new car design early next year. This is causing a lot of excitement in the auto industry." [The announcement . . .]

The announcement that Volkswagen would unveil a new car design early next year is causing a lot of excitement in the auto industry.

1. "The Health Ministry announced that they will begin vaccinating all infants for measles. This was greeted with criticism from the opposition party." [The announcement . . .]
2. "The president said it was possible that he would resign by the end of this year. This has taken everyone by surprise, including the news media." [The possibility . . .]
3. "The *London Sun* reported that Dr. Regina Blair of the Glasgow Medical Center has discovered a new protein. This is attracting much interest in the world of science." [The report . . .]
4. "The *Auckland Times* claimed that a 95-year-old New Zealand man had broken the world record for growing the longest beard. This has triggered similar claims across three continents." [The claim . . .]

Unit 3

The future continuous

Use the future continuous for actions that will be in progress at a specific time or over a period of time in the future.
To form the future continuous, use <u>will</u> + <u>be</u> + a present participle OR <u>be going to</u> + <u>be</u> + a present participle.

At this time next week, I { 'll be lying / 'm going to be lying } on a beach in Hawaii. [specific time]

I { 'll be studying / 'm going to be studying } English in the United States for about two years. [period of time]

Sometimes sentences in the simple future and the future continuous have almost the same meaning. Choose the future continuous to emphasize a continuous or uninterrupted activity.
Next year, I'll study English in the United States.
Next year, I'll be studying English in the United States.

Questions and short answers
Will you be working at home? Yes, I will. / No, I won't.
Are you going to be working at home? Yes, I am. / No, I'm not.

Use the future continuous and a time clause with <u>while</u> or <u>when</u> to describe a continuous activity that will occur at the same time as another activity. Do not use a future form in the time clause.
I'll be looking for a job while my wife continues her studies.
NOT I'll be looking for a job while my wife will be continuing her studies.

When the mayor is speaking, we'll be listening carefully.
NOT When the mayor will be speaking, we'll be listening carefully.

> **REMEMBER**
>
> Stative verbs are "non-action" verbs such as <u>be</u>, <u>have</u>, <u>know</u>, <u>remember</u>, <u>like</u>, <u>seem</u>, <u>appreciate</u>, etc.
>
> **Do not use the continuous with stative verbs.**
> DON'T SAY By next month, I'll be having a new car.
>
> **For a complete list of stative verbs, see page A3 in the Appendices.**

A On a separate sheet of paper, correct the errors in the following sentences.

1. She'll be staying at the Newton Hotel when she's going to be attending the meeting.
2. We won't be spending much time sightseeing while we'll be visiting London.
3. When he's going to stay in town, he's going to be meeting with some friends.
4. She'll be correcting homework while the students will be taking the test.
5. While Michelle will be serving dessert, Randy will already be washing the dishes.
6. Won't they be going to sleep in New York when you'll be getting up in Taipei?

B Complete the following sentences, using the future continuous with <u>will</u> when possible. If the future continuous is not possible, use the simple future with <u>will</u>.

1. After I've completed my studies, I .... for a job.
   (look)

2. She .... historic sites while she's in Turkey.
   (photograph)

3. In a few years, they .... all the problems they had.
   (not / remember)

4. .... he .... between flights for very long?
   (wait)

5. I'm sure she .... when you call.
   (not / sleep)

The future perfect continuous

Use the future perfect continuous to emphasize the continuous quality of an action that began before a specific time in the future. To form the future perfect continuous, use <u>will</u> + <u>have</u> + <u>been</u> and a present participle.

By next year, I'**ll have been studying** English for five years. [Describes an action that began before "next year" and may still continue.]

Combine a statement using the future perfect continuous with a time clause to show the relationship between two future actions. Use the simple present tense in the time clause.

By the time I **arrive** in New York, I'**ll have been sitting** in a plane for over ten hours.
NOT By the time I'll arrive in New York, I'll have been sitting in a plane for over ten hours.

C Complete the notecard, using the future continuous or the future perfect continuous.

Dear Ida,

Venice was great, but finally on to Paris! By tomorrow afternoon, I .... down
(1. stroll)
the Champs Elysées and .... in
(2. take)
the beautiful sights of that great city. In the evening, I .... an opera by Bizet
(3. enjoy)
in the city where he was born. Just think, by Saturday, I .... delicious French
(4. eat)
food for a whole week! Plus, I ....
(5. practice)
my French with real native speakers.

Then, after Paris, it's off to the Riviera, where
I .... around on the beaches of
(6. lounge)
Nice and Saint-Tropez for a week. By that time,
I .... for three weeks, and it will
(7. travel)
almost be time to come home—a long trip for a homebody like me!

See you soon!

Pavel

Unit 4

A **Review.** Check *all* the quantifiers that can complete each sentence correctly.

1. If a child watches .... television, he or she may develop a self-image problem.
   ☐ a lot of   ☐ several   ☐ a number of   ☐ a great deal of

2. I don't think you can say that .... young people are self-conscious about their bodies.
   ☐ most   ☐ a great deal of   ☐ every   ☐ a majority of

3. It's clear that .... company needs to make its own decision about it.
   ☐ some   ☐ each   ☐ every   ☐ most

4. There are .... beauty treatments available to our customers.
   ☐ a number of   ☐ a few   ☐ plenty of   ☐ a little

5. I was surprised to read that .... men are considering cosmetic surgery.
   ☐ a lot of   ☐ some   ☐ every   ☐ less

Quantifiers: <u>a few</u> and <u>few</u>, <u>a little</u> and <u>little</u>

Use <u>a few</u> with plural count nouns and <u>a little</u> with non-count nouns to mean "some." Use <u>few</u> with plural count nouns and <u>little</u> with non-count nouns to mean "not many" or "not much."

A few companies are allowing their employees to dress casually on Fridays. [some companies]

Few companies are allowing their employees to dress casually on Fridays. [not many companies]

Employees are showing **a little interest** in this new dress code. [some interest]

Employees are showing **little interest** in this new dress code. [not much interest]

B Change the underlined quantifiers to <u>a few</u>, <u>few</u>, <u>a little</u>, or <u>little</u>.

a little

Example: Would you like to listen to ~~some~~ music?

1. We actually eat <u>almost no</u> meat.

2. The newspaper had <u>a bit of</u> information about the concert tonight.

3. There were <u>several</u> new students in my class today.

4. To tell the truth, I've seen <u>hardly any</u> movies in the last month.

5. I enjoy visiting my hometown, but there's <u>not much</u> to do there.

6. If you look in the refrigerator, there should be <u>some</u> eggs.

Quantifiers: using <u>of</u>

Use <u>of</u> (to refer to something specific) when a noun is preceded by a possessive adjective, a possessive noun, a demonstrative pronoun, or the article <u>the</u>.

most of Jack's co-workers	–	**most** co-workers in Italy
several of these companies	–	**several** companies
a few of the choices	–	**a few** choices
a little of the cake	–	**a little** cake
many of those books	–	**many** books
any of her friends	–	**any** friends
much of the coffee	–	**much** coffee
some of his students	–	**some** students
each of the classes	–	**each** class
one of my cats	–	**one** cat
all of our employees	–	**all** employees

possessive adjectives my, her, their, etc.
possessive nouns John's, the doctor's
demonstrative pronouns this, that, these, those

BE CAREFUL! In the superlative, do not use <u>of</u> with <u>most</u>.
DON'T SAY Tokyo is the city with the most ~~of~~ people in Japan.

Using <u>of</u> after <u>all</u> or <u>both</u> is optional, with no change in meaning.

all of our employees	OR	**all** our employees	NOT	all ~~of~~ employees
both of those choices	OR	**both** those choices	NOT	both ~~of~~ choices

BE CAREFUL! <u>Of</u> must be included when using an object pronoun.
both of them NOT ~~both them~~

<u>One</u> and <u>each</u> are used with singular nouns only. But <u>one of</u> and <u>each of</u> are used with plural nouns only. However, the meaning of both expressions is still singular.

One student	–	**One of** the students
Each class	–	**Each of** the classes

Some quantifiers must include <u>of</u> when they modify a noun or noun phrase.

a lot of	a majority of
lots of	plenty of
a couple of	a bit of
a number of	a great deal of

C Only one of each pair of sentences is correct. Check the correct sentence and correct the mistake in the other one.

      Example: **a.** ✔ She went with several of her classmates.

            b. _____ Several ~~of~~ classmates went out for coffee.

  1. **a.** _____ Most of companies in the world are fairly formal.

      b. _____ Most of the companies in the United States have dress-down days.

  2. **a.** _____ All of hot appetizers were delicious.

      b. _____ Everyone tried all of the cold appetizers.

  3. **a.** _____ A lot of my friends have traveled to exotic places.

      b. _____ There are a lot places I'd like to see.

  4. **a.** _____ I read a few of Steinbeck's novels last year.

      b. _____ A few of novels by Steinbeck take place in Mexico.

  5. **a.** _____ Several managers were interviewed, and many them liked the new policy.

      b. _____ Many of the employees we spoke with liked the new policy.

Quantifiers: used without referents

Most quantifiers can be used without the noun they describe as long as the context has been made clear earlier.

   A number of people believe there is life on other planets. But **many** don't. [many people]

Grammar for Writing: subject-verb agreement with quantifiers with _of_

In quantifiers with _of_, the verb must agree with the noun that comes after _of_.
   Some of the movie is in English. – Some of the movies are in English.
   A lot of the music was jazz. – A lot of the musicians were young.

In formal English, _none of_ is followed by a singular verb. However, in everyday spoken English, it is common to use it with a plural verb.
   Formal: None of the students was late for class.
   Informal: None of the students were late for class.

> **BE CAREFUL!** The quantifiers <u>one of</u>, <u>each of</u>, and <u>every one of</u> are always followed by a plural noun, but they always take a singular verb.
>   One of the students <u>likes</u> rap music.

D Choose the verb that agrees with each subject.

  1. Every one of these choices (sound / **sounds**) terrific!

  2. One of the teachers (was / were) going to stay after class.

  3. A lot of the problem (is / are) that no one wants to work so hard.

  4. Each of the employees (want / wants) to work overtime.

  5. Half of the city (was / were) flooded in the storm.

  6. None of the players (is coming / are coming) to the game.

  7. Only 8 percent of their workers prefer shorter work weeks, while at least 90 percent (don't / doesn't).

Unit 5

Conjunctions with so, too, neither, or not either

Use <u>and so</u> or <u>and . . . too</u> to join affirmative statements that are similar.
  Spitting on the street is offensive, **and so** is littering.
  OR Spitting on the street is offensive, **and** littering is **too**.

Use <u>neither</u> or <u>not either</u> to join negative statements that are similar.
  Spitting on the street doesn't bother me, **and neither** does littering.
  Spitting on the street doesn't bother me, **and** littering doesn't **either**.

If the first clause uses the verb **be**, an auxiliary verb, or a modal,
use the same structure in the second clause.
  Tokyo **is** a huge city, and so **is** São Paulo.
  New York **doesn't** have a lot of industry, and neither **does** London.
  Mexico City **has** grown a lot, and so **has** Los Angeles.
  Nancy **can't** tolerate loud radios, and neither **can** Tom.

If the first clause does not include the verb **be**, an auxiliary verb, or
a modal, use a form of **do**.
  John **thinks** graffiti is a big problem, and so **does** Helen.

> **BE CAREFUL!** Use a negative with
> <u>either</u> and an affirmative with <u>neither</u>.
>   . . . and neither does littering.
>   NOT . . . and neither ~~doesn't~~ littering.
>   . . . and littering doesn't either.
>   NOT . . . and littering ~~does either~~.

> **BE CAREFUL!** Notice the subject-verb order.
>   . . . and so is littering.
>   . . . and littering is too.
>   . . . and neither does littering.
>   . . . and littering doesn't either.

> **BE CAREFUL!** With <u>so</u> and <u>neither</u>, the verb (or auxiliary
> verb) goes before the subject.
>   Nancy can't stand loud boom boxes, and neither can Tom.
>   NOT . . . neither ~~Tom can~~.
>   Tokyo is a huge city, and so is São Paulo.
>   NOT . . . and so ~~São Paulo is~~.

A Find and underline the nine errors. On a separate sheet of paper, write each sentence correctly.

New York is one of the most famous cities in the world, and so does London. While these two cities differ in many ways, they also share a number of characteristics. Here's a quick comparison:

- If you're looking for peace and quiet, New York is not the place to be, and neither London is. They are both exciting and noisy places. If you're not used to it, New York's traffic can be deafening at times, and so does London's.
- The best way to get around in both cities is the subway (or the Tube in London). New York's subway system is quite old and elaborate, and is London's too.

- If you're looking for first-rate entertainment, New York is filled with theaters, and so London does.
- Hungry? London's restaurants feature exciting dishes from around the world, and New York's are too.
- Both cities offer a huge choice of museums to visit. The museums in New York can't possibly be seen in a day, and either London's can't.
- New York offers some of the world's most famous tourist sites—for example, the Statue of Liberty and the Empire State Building—and so is London, with Buckingham Palace and the Millennium Wheel.

It's clear that New York shouldn't be missed, and neither London shouldn't!

B On a separate sheet of paper, rewrite each statement, using the word in parentheses. Make any necessary changes in verbs or possessive adjectives.

Example: Both Vilnius and Riga have large historic districts. (so)

Vilnius has a large historic district, and so does Riga.

1. Both Bangkok and São Paulo face many problems caused by too much traffic. (so)
2. Both Athens and Barcelona have hosted the Olympic Games in the past. (too)
3. Vancouver and Taipei don't ever get very cold. (neither)
4. Mexico City and Tokyo won't experience a decrease in their populations any time soon. (not either)
5. Both Hong Kong and Rio de Janeiro are famous for their physical beauty. (so)
6. Prague and Krakow attract people who like great architecture. (too)
7. The Prado Museum in Madrid and the Louvre in Paris shouldn't be missed. (neither)
8. Tokyo and Mexico City haven't lost their places among the world's largest cities yet. (not either)

So, too, neither, or not either: short responses

Use so, too, neither, or not either in short responses to express agreement.

A: I hate littering.   B: **So** do I. / I do **too**.   NOT So do I ~~hate~~. / I do ~~hate~~ too.

A: I can't stand smoking.   B: I can't **either**. / **Neither** can I.   NOT I can't ~~stand~~ either. / Neither can I ~~stand~~.

In English, it is common to express agreement with me too or me neither.

A: I hate littering.   B: **Me too.**

A: I can't stand smoking.   B: **Me neither.**

C Agree with each statement. Use short responses with so, too, neither, or not either.

1. A: I've never been to Ulan Bator.   **B:** ....

2. A: I can't figure this out.   **B:** ....

3. A: I loved going there!   **B:** ....

4. A: I have to get some cash.   **B:** ....

5. A: I'm getting really tired.   **B:** ....

6. A: I used to travel more.   **B:** ....

7. A: I'll call her tomorrow.   **B:** ....

8. A: I'm not going to tell her she's late.   **B:** ....

Unit 6

Modals and modal-like expressions: summary

Make polite requests

Could I get your phone number?

Can my son have just one more cookie?

Would you please hold this for a second? (with you only)

May I have a cup of coffee? (with I or we only, formal)

Express preferences

I **would like to** see that movie.

Would you **like to** go running?

I'd **rather not** see a movie.

I **would rather** have left earlier.

Give or ask for permission

You **can** open the window if you want.

Can I leave this here?

You **may** leave early if you need to.

May I leave my coat here? (with I or we only, formal)

Express ability or lack of ability

He **can** complete the job for you in an hour.

Can you write well in English?

We **couldn't** finish the report yesterday.

Couldn't you find the restaurant?

My grandmother **isn't able to** walk any more.

Is she **able to** take care of herself?

She **was able to** do a lot more when she was younger.

Express possibility

It **may** rain this afternoon.

He **may not** be able to come this morning.

She **may** have forgotten to lock the door.

She **may not** have remembered.

It **might** be noisy at that restaurant.

She **might not** want to eat anything.

He **might** have gone home already.

He **might not** have paid yet.

Draw conclusions

Your father **must** be very smart.

She **must not** think it's important.

They **must** have been exhausted when they got home.

He **must not** have sent it.

Suggest alternatives

You **could** take the next train.

She **could** have bought it for less.

Give suggestions

They really **should** think about staying longer.

He **shouldn't** have waited to make a reservation.

They **should** have called first.

You **shouldn't** stay at that hotel.

They really **ought to** think about staying longer.

They **ought to** have called first.

Should we have called first?

NOTE: Ought to is not usually used in negative statements or questions. Use shouldn't or should instead.

Give a warning

Your mother **had better** see a doctor right away.
You **had better not** forget about your appointment.
He **had better** have called this morning.
They **had better not** have hurt any animals when they
    made that movie.

> NOTE: <u>Had better</u> is generally not used in
> questions. In spoken English, the contraction
> <u>'d better</u> is almost always used.

Express necessity

All students **have to** take the test.
All students **must** take the test. [formal]
All students **have got to** take the test. [spoken only]

Express lack of necessity

You **don't have to** have a passport.
She **didn't have to** pay a late fee.

Express prohibition or deny permission

New employees **shouldn't** park their cars in the garage.
New employees **cannot** park their cars in the garage.
New employees **must not** park their cars in the garage. [formal]
New employees **may not** park their cars in the garage. [formal]

> NOTE: In questions, <u>have to</u> is generally used.
> Questions with <u>must</u> are very formal and not very
> common. Past necessity is expressed with <u>had to</u>.
> **Does** everyone **have to** take the test?
> **Must** everyone take the test?
> All students **had to** take the test.

A Cross out the one modal that *cannot* be used in each sentence or question.

1. (May / Can / Could) your mother please call me tonight?

2. I (wasn't able to / couldn't / shouldn't) get there on time because the traffic was so bad.

3. She (may / had better / can) be able to complete the job by tomorrow.

4. (Can / Should / Ought to) my students listen in while you practice?

5. Shoppers (may / have to / must) not load their cars in front of the main entrance.

6. Thank goodness she (doesn't have to / must not / was able to) renew her passport for another five years.

8. You (could / had better / should) let his assistant know you won't be able to make it on time, or you may not get the job.

9. This restaurant is so good we (ought to / might / would rather) come here more often.

B Circle the one modal that best completes each conversation.

1. **A:** Why didn't you come to the party last night?
   B: I (had to / have to / must / have got to) study for a test.

2. **A:** You really (can't / should / mustn't / are able to) call more often.
   B: You're right. I'm sorry.

3. **A:** She ('d better not have / should have / had to have / must have) forgotten the tickets!
   B: Uh-oh. I hate to tell you this, but I think she did.

4. **A:** Do you think I ('m able to / must / would / could) get your phone number?
   B: Sure.

5. **A:** Did you get to go to the movies?
   B: Yeah. But I (must have / 'd rather have / should not have / would have) stayed at home.

6. **A:** Unfortunately, the doctor (shouldn't / has to / won't be able to / had better) see you until tomorrow.
   B: That's OK. No problem.

7. **A:** What do you think happened to Judy?
   B: She (must not have / shouldn't have / isn't able to / didn't have to) known we were starting so early.

Unit 7

Grammar for Writing: past forms of gerunds and infinitives

Gerunds and infinitives have past forms to express actions that occurred in the past.

I appreciate **having had** the opportunity to meet our overseas colleagues.
They were disappointed **not to have met** everyone from the Jakarta office.
We didn't mind **having been delayed** so long in Paris.
He's surprised **to have heard** about your resignation.

If the main verb is in the simple past tense or the past of <u>be</u>, the gerund or infinitive can be in either the present or past form, with no change in meaning. It is more common to use the present form of a gerund or an infinitive in everyday spoken English.

They were disappointed **not to meet** everyone from the Jakarta office.
We didn't mind **being delayed** so long in Paris.

Past forms	
Active voice	
gerund	<u>having</u> + past participle
infinitive	<u>to have</u> + past participle
Passive voice	
gerund	<u>having been</u> + past participle
infinitive	<u>to have been</u> + past participle

A Use a past gerund or infinitive form of each verb to complete the statements. Use the passive voice where necessary. Refer to page A3 in the Appendices if necessary.

1. It was clear that many passengers were shocked about .... from the flight without
   (bump)
   warning.

2. The ministers were found guilty of .... personal gifts from foreign companies.
   (accept)

3. At the news conference, the president mentioned .... with his advisers about the
   (speak)
   problem.

4. The mayor apologized today for .... immediately to the disaster.
   (not / respond)

5. Most of the seniors expressed their happiness at .... as participants in the event.
   (choose)

6. They were accused of .... money from the cash register.
   (take)

7. The newspaper reporter appeared .... by a government worker who claimed she knew
   (contact)
   what had really happened.

8. We want you to know how much we regret .... such a serious mistake.
   (make)

Unit 8

Making comparisons: summary

Comparative forms of adjectives and adverbs show how two things are different.

John is **taller than** Rob (is).
This movie was **less interesting than** the last one (was).
My sister types **a lot faster than** I (do).
There is **less corruption** in the government **than** there used to be.

Superlative forms of adjectives and adverbs show how one thing is different from everything else.

She was **the nicest person** I ever met!
That was **the least entertaining** movie I ever saw.
Of all the actors, she sang **the most beautifully.**
Among my friends, Ned and Stacey definitely have **the most money.**
Of all the cars we looked at, the Linkus **costs the most.**

> **BE CAREFUL!** Use <u>the</u> with a superlative form. However, you can omit <u>the</u> if the superlative is not followed by a noun.
> Which student is **the tallest** OR **tallest?**
> NOT ~~Which is tallest student?~~

Comparisons with <u>as . . . as</u> show how two things are alike.

Tom is just **as tall as** George (is).
She still sings **as beautifully as** she did when she was young.
My nephew now **weighs as much as** I do.
I have **as much money** in the bank **as** I did last year.

Use <u>as . . . as</u> with <u>almost</u>, <u>about</u>, and <u>not quite</u> to show how two things are similar, but not equal.

My nephew weighs **almost as much as** I do.
  [I weigh a bit more.]
The movie is **about as** long as his last one.
  [But it's a bit shorter.]
This coat **isn't quite as** expensive **as** it looks.
  [It's actually cheaper.]

Use <u>as . . . as</u> with <u>twice</u>, <u>three times</u>, etc., to show that things are not equal at all.

A Linkus sedan is about **twice as** expensive **as** a Matsu.
My new computer is **ten times as** fast **as** my old one.

Irregular forms

adjective	adverb	comparative	superlative
good	well	better (than)	the best
bad	badly	worse (than)	the worst
far	far	farther / further (than)	the farthest / furthest
a little	a little	less (than)	the least
a few	a few	fewer (than)	the fewest
many / a lot of	—	more (than)	the most
much / a lot of	—	much / a lot more (than)	the most

NOTE: In informal spoken English, it is more common to say ". . . as tall as me" instead of the more formal ". . . as tall as I."

A Read each quoted statement. Then complete each sentence using a comparative, superlative, or comparison with <u>as . . . as</u>.

1. "The textbook we are using now is very good. The textbook we were using last year was also very good."

   The textbook we're using now is _____ the one we were using last year.

2. "Star shampoo costs about $6.00. Ravel shampoo costs about $7.00. Sanabel shampoo costs about $5.00."

   Among the three shampoos, Sanabel is _____ .

3. "We paid four hundred euros each for our tickets. They paid three hundred euros."

   We paid _____ they did.

4. "Hank has only a little experience working with children. Nancy has a lot of experience."

   Hank has _____ Nancy.

5. "John's laptop weighs 4 kilos. Gerry's laptop weighs 4.1 kilos."

   John's laptop isn't _____ Gerry's is.

6. "Mark knows only a little Japanese. Jonah knows a lot."

   Mark knows _____ Jonah does.

7. "Bart ate a lot for lunch. Susan ate a lot for lunch too."

   Susan ate _____ Bart did for lunch.

Other uses of comparatives, superlatives, and comparisons with as ... as

For emphasis

The Nile River is **more than** 5,500 kilometers long. [emphasizes that the river is very long]

The Dickens School now has **fewer than** 900 students. [emphasizes that this is a relatively small number]

A newborn Asian elephant can weigh **as much as** 150 kilos. [emphasizes that this is fairly heavy]

As many as 200 of these animals are killed every year. [emphasizes that this is a high number]

That was **the worst** movie **ever**. [emphasizes that this was a bad movie]

This meal was **the best ever**! [emphasizes that this was a great meal]

To show progression

My son is getting **taller** every day. [He's growing.]

The economy is **stronger** now. [It's improving.]

To show tendencies or preferences

We eat out **more than** in. [We tend to eat out.]

Sara likes being alone **more than** socializing. [She prefers to spend time alone.]

To clarify

He's a lot **friendlier than** you would think. [You may think he's not friendly, but in fact he is.]

She's **more of a singer than** a dancer. [People may think she's mainly a dancer, but in fact she's mainly a singer.]

The movie's **more annoying than** scary. [You may think this movie will be scary, but in fact it's just annoying.]

It looks **more like** snow **than** rain. [You may think it's going to rain, but in fact it looks like it's going to snow.]

B Use a comparative, a superlative, or a comparison with <u>as ... as</u> to complete each statement so it has a similar meaning to the information in quotes.

1. "Our meal last night was really inexpensive. It only cost 48 euros for the two of us."

   Our meal last night cost .... 50 euros.

2. "Our reading club meetings are getting pretty big. On some nights there are thirty students."

   Our reading club meetings sometimes have .... students.

3. "I think our teacher is really great!"

   Our teacher is .... ever!

4. "The garden you planted last month has become so beautiful!"

   Your garden is getting .... every day!

5. "You may think snails might taste strange, but they actually taste quite good."

   Snails taste .... you may think.

6. "You may think Kate is shy, but she's actually very talkative."

   Kate is .... than you might think.

Unit 9

Say, ask, and tell: summary

Say and ask are the most common reporting verbs in direct speech. Use say for statements and ask for questions.

"I completely disagree with the president on this issue," **said** the education minister.

"Who do they think is in control of this government?" **asked** the president.

Note the use of say, ask, and tell in indirect speech.

She **said** (to the press) that she completely disagreed with the president.

She **asked** (the press) if they disagreed with the president.

She **told** the press that she completely disagreed with the president.

BE CAREFUL!

DON'T SAY She ~~said the press~~ that she completely disagreed with the president.

DON'T SAY She ~~told~~ that she completely disagreed with the president.

DON'T SAY She ~~told to the press~~ that she completely disagreed with the president.

A Complete the sentences with a form of <u>say</u>, <u>ask</u>, or <u>tell</u>.

1. She .... the waiter if she could pay with a credit card.
2. We .... that we would come back later when they were less busy.
3. He .... his friends that he would be a few minutes late.
4. She .... to her teacher that she needed a bit more time.
5. I .... my kids whether they would mind if we stopped at the store on the way home.
6. They .... the reporter that they were ready to provide information about the case.
7. He .... to the clerk that it was the longest he'd ever had to wait on line.
8. I .... them if they enjoyed the movie.

Grammar for Writing: other reporting verbs

Writers use a variety of reporting verbs to describe actions more specifically and accurately.

argue
"Things are definitely getting worse," **argues** Charles Wilder, a leading economic advisor to the president.
Charles Wilder, a leading economic advisor to the president, **argues** that things are getting worse.

claim
"Baylor was taking bribes," **claims** the *Daily Sun*.
The *Daily Sun* **claims** that Baylor was taking bribes.

declare
"The mayor has been doing a brilliant job!" **declared** the governor on Tuesday.
On Tuesday, the governor **declared** that the mayor had been doing a brilliant job.

explain
"You should always discuss dieting with your doctor," Dr. Fish **explained**.
Dr. Fish **explained** that people should always discuss dieting with their doctors.

report
The New York Times **reports**, "Obesity is a growing problem in Asia."
Last year, *The New York Times* **reported** that obesity was a growing problem in Asia.

state
The new CEO **stated**, "Things are going to change around here."
The new CEO **stated** that things were going to change at the company.

More reporting verbs	
add	maintain
announce	mention
answer	promise
comment	remark
complain	reply
exclaim	reveal
imply	write

B On a separate sheet of paper, restate each sentence with a different reporting verb. Use a dictionary if necessary.

1. The *Bangkok Post* says that the president of Chile will be visiting Thailand next month.
2. The minister of education said yesterday that major improvements have been made in schools across the country.
3. The secretary of the United Nations says that more should be done to alleviate world hunger.
4. The scientists who conducted the study said that more research would have to be conducted.
5. The children who wrote on the walls said that they wouldn't do it again.
6. The BBC said that it would increase its coverage of the news in the Middle East.

Unit 10

Intensifiers

Adverbs of degree, also called "intensifiers," modify adjectives and add emphasis.

An intensifier goes before a modifying adjective or series of modifying adjectives.
   a **really** interesting book
   a **considerably** large round orange

Intensifiers	
really	somewhat
very	fairly
pretty*	slightly
extremely	wonderfully
rather	considerably

*informal spoken

A   Complete the restaurant review with appropriate intensifiers.

> *Chez Pierre: Fine dining at its best!*
>   Upon arriving at this .... lovely restaurant, guests are greeted by Chef Pierre, who proudly explains the .... impressive new menu. There are some .... inexpensive dinner choices that are sure to satisfy even the most demanding diners. The elegant European-style décor at Chez Pierre only adds to the experience. However, the .... subdued lighting makes it hard to read the menu and is .... disappointing. Be sure to ask about their .... extensive dessert choices, which don't require good lighting for you to enjoy them thoroughly!

Adverbs of manner

Adverbs of manner show how something is done or happens. They usually go at the end of a clause when the adverb provides important information in the sentence.
   He ate his dinner **slowly**.   She sings really **well**.

Adverbs of manner ending in –ly can go before the verb or verb phrase when they are not the main focus of the sentence.
   I **slowly** opened the door. [focus is on opening the door]
   I opened the door **slowly**. [focus is on how the door was opened]
   He **angrily** hung up the phone. [focus is on hanging up the phone]
   He hung up the phone **angrily**. [focus is on how the phone was hung up]

Adverbs of manner can go before the past participle in the passive voice.
   His report was very **poorly** written.

BE CAREFUL! Do not place an adverb of manner between a verb and a direct object.
   He drank his coffee **quickly**.   NOT   He drank ~~quickly~~ his coffee.

Adverbs of manner	
angrily	poorly
badly	quietly
fast	sadly
happily	slowly
hard	softly
nicely	suddenly
noisily	well

B   Check if the adverb is correctly used. If not, make corrections.

   ☐ **1.** When the game was over, he left quickly the court.

   ☐ **2.** As she drove into town, she sang to herself softly.

   ☐ **3.** The meeting was suddenly postponed after the CEO arrived.

   ☐ **4.** They pretended noisily to wash the dinner dishes as they listened in on the conversation.

   ☐ **5.** He congratulated her for her nicely presented report.

   ☐ **6.** They entered quietly the room and sat in the corner.

Pronunciation Booster

The *Pronunciation Booster* is optional. It provides more information about pronunciation as well as additional practice. The exercises can be found on both the Class Audio Program and the Student's Take-Home Audio CD.

Unit 1

Content words and function words

In English, content words are generally stressed.
Function words are generally unstressed.

My **BOSS** is a **PAIN** in the **NECK**!
He's **REALLY** a **TERRIFIC BOSS**.
MARK is such a **SMART GUY**.
I'm **SURE** she'll be a **GREAT MANAGER**.

Stress in compound nouns

A compound noun is a noun that is made up of two or more words.
Stress generally falls on the first word in compound nouns.

compound noun		adjective + noun
He's a **WISE** guy.	BUT	He's a **WISE LEADER**.
She's a **PEOPLE** person.	BUT	She's a **NICE PERSON**.
It's an **APARTMENT** building.	BUT	It's a **TALL BUILDING**.
They're **EXERCISE** machines.	BUT	They're **NEW MACHINES**.

Content words

nouns	boss, Julie, happiness
verbs	find, meet, call
adjectives	talkative, small, green
adverbs	quietly, again, slowly
possessive pronouns	mine, yours, his
demonstrative pronouns	this, those, that
reflexive pronouns	ourselves, herself
interrogative pronouns	what, who, where

Function words

prepositions	of, from, at
conjunctions	and, but, or
determiners	a, the, some
personal pronouns	he, she, they
possessive adjectives	my, her, their
auxiliary verbs	have + [past participle]
	be + [present participle]

BE CAREFUL! When an auxiliary verb is negative or used in short answers, it is generally stressed.
I **CAN'T GO.**   He **WON'T LIKE** it.
No, they **DON'T**.   Yes, I **HAVE.**

A 🎧 Listen and practice.

1. My **BOSS** is a **PAIN** in the **NECK**!
2. He's **REALLY** a **TERRIFIC BOSS**.
3. **MARK** is such a **SMART GUY**.
4. I'm **SURE** she'll be a **GREAT MANAGER**.

B Circle the content words.

1. Learn to live in the present.
2. He reminded me to call my mother.
3. He asked me to work faster.
4. I prefer to stick closer to home.

🎧 Now practice reading each sentence aloud and listen to compare.* (Note that your choices may differ from what you hear on the audio.)

C 🎧 Listen and practice.

1. He's a **WISE** guy.   He's a **WISE LEADER**.
2. She's a **PEOPLE** person.   She's a **NICE PERSON**.
3. It's an **APARTMENT** building.   It's a **TALL BUILDING**.
4. They're **EXERCISE** machines.   They're **NEW MACHINES**.

D 🎧 Practice reading each compound noun aloud and listen to check.*

1. a swimming pool
2. tennis courts
3. an answering machine
4. a telephone directory
5. office managers
6. the bullet train

*NOTE: Whenever you see a listening activity with an asterisk (*), say each word, phrase, or sentence in the pause *after* each number. Then listen for confirmation.

Unit 2

Intonation patterns

In statements, commands, and information questions, lower pitch after the stressed syllable in the last stressed word. If the last syllable in the sentence is stressed, lower pitch on the vowel by lengthening it.

I haven't been to many concerts lately.   Don't forget to watch them on TV tonight.

What do you like about that song?

Raise pitch after the stressed syllable in the last stressed word in <u>yes</u> / <u>no</u> questions and requests. If the last syllable in the sentence is stressed, raise pitch on the vowel by lengthening it.

Have you ever heard of Annie Lennox?   Could you pick up their new CD for me?

Do you think she has a nice voice?

A 🎧 Listen and practice.

1. I haven't been to many concerts lately.
2. Don't forget to watch them on TV tonight.
3. What do you like about that song?
4. Have you ever heard of Annie Lennox?
5. Could you pick up their new CD for me?
6. Do you think she has a nice voice?

B Circle the last stressed content word in each of the following sentences. If that word has more than one syllable, underline the stressed syllable.

1. That song has a great beat you can dance to.
2. Her catchy lyrics make you want to sing along.
3. Didn't you like that song's melody?
4. What time do you think the concert will be finished?

🎧 Now practice reading each sentence aloud, using the intonation patterns you have learned. Listen to check.*

Unit 3

Sentence rhythm: thought groups

Longer sentences are usually divided by rhythm into smaller "thought groups" —groups of words that naturally or logically go together. Exactly how statements may be divided into thought groups will vary among speakers.

Examples of thought groups	
subject + verb	I don't know
noun phrases	my short-term goal
prepositional phrases	by the end of the month
predicates	is drowning in debt
noun clauses	where the money goes
adjective clauses	that I paid off last year
adverbial clauses	when I've finished my report

My short-term goal / is to start living / within my means.
NOT ~~My short-term / goal is to / start living within my / means.~~
I don't plan / to be financially dependent / for the rest of my life.
By next year / I hope to have gotten / a good job / as a financial consultant.

Pitch in longer sentences

In longer sentences, pitch may fall—or rise—after the last stressed syllable in each thought group, with no change in meaning.

Once he tries keeping / a realistic budget / he'll find it easy / to save money. **OR**

Once he tries keeping / a realistic budget / he'll find it easy / to save money.

A 🎧 Listen and practice.

  1. My short-term goal is to start living within my means.
  2. I don't plan to be financially dependent for the rest of my life.
  3. By next year, I hope to have gotten a good job as a financial consultant.
  4a. Once he tries keeping a realistic budget, he'll find it easy to save money.
  4b. Once he tries keeping a realistic budget, he'll find it easy to save money.

B Read the following sentences. Decide how you might break each sentence into thought groups.

  1. By the end of this month, I hope to have finished paying off my student loans.
  2. In two months, when we've finally paid off our house, we're going to have a big party to celebrate.
  3. To be perfectly honest, I couldn't tell you where the money goes.
  4. By next year, I will have completed my studies, but I don't think I will have gotten married.

  🎧 Now practice reading each sentence aloud, paying attention to pitch. Listen to compare.*
(Note that your choices may differ from what you hear on the audio.)

Unit 4

Linking sounds

Linking with vowels

When the final consonant sound of a word is followed by a vowel sound, link the sounds together.

It's in style now.
She bought him an elegant tie.
I've already bought a new suit.

Linking identical consonants

When the final consonant sound of a word is followed by the same sound, link the sounds together as one sound.

She thinks the blouse is striking.
They preferred dark suits.
What an attractive vest!

A 🎧 Listen and practice.

1. It's in style now.
2. She bought him an elegant tie.
3. I've already bought a new suit.
4. She thinks the blouse is striking.
5. They preferred dark suits.
6. What an attractive vest!

B Underline all the places where you think the sounds should be linked.

1. She wants Susan to dress up next time.
2. It's fashionable and elegant.
3. It's out of style.
4. I wish she preferred dressing down.
5. That blouse isn't trendy enough for my taste.
6. I think Kyle has stylish taste.

🎧 Now practice reading each sentence aloud and listen to check.*

Unit 5

Unstressed syllables: vowel reduction to /ə/

In conversation, the vowels in unstressed syllables are often reduced to the sound /ə/. The vowel sound /ə/ occurs more often in English than any other vowel sound and contributes to maintaining the rhythm of English.

ac cept a ble → /ək'sɛptəbəl/	re spect ful → /rə'spɛkʧəl/
con sid er ate → /kən'sɪdərət/	ir re spon si ble → /ˌɪrə'spɑnsəbəl/
po lite → /pə'laɪt/	in ex cus a ble → /ˌɪnək'skyuzəbəl/

A 🎧 Listen and practice.

1. acceptable
2. considerate
3. polite
4. respectful
5. irresponsible
6. inexcusable

B 🎧 Listen to each word and circle the unstressed syllables that have the sound /ə/.

1. un ac cept a ble
2. in con si de rate
3. im po lite
4. un pleas ant
5. ir ra tion al
6. im ma ture
7. un i mag i na ble
8. dis re spect ful
9. in ap pro pri ate

🎧 Now practice reading each word aloud and listen again to check.*

P4

Unit 6

Sound reduction

In everyday speech, sounds in unstressed words are often "reduced"; that is, vowels change to /ə/ or /ɚ/ or consonants are dropped.

Vowel reduction

The /u/ sound in the function word <u>to</u> is often reduced to /ə/.

I'll be going **to** the airport after dinner. /tə/

It's ten **to** two. /tə/

The /æ/ sound in many one-syllable function words is often reduced to /ə/.

Look **at** that. /ət/

I got **an** iguana. /ən/

That's more **than** I need. /ðən/

The /ɑr/ and /ɔr/ sounds in function words are often reduced to /ɚ/.

Pets **are** no trouble. /ɚ/

Is it black **or** white? /ɚ/

Where's **your** farm? /yɚ/

He's been gone **for** days. /fɚ/

> **BE CAREFUL!** Function words that occur at the end of a sentence are never reduced.
>
> What a beautiful bird you **are**! /ɑr/
>
> What are you looking **at**? /æt/
>
> What are you waiting **for**? /fɔr/
>
> Who's she talking **to**? /tu/

The function word <u>and</u> /ænd/ is often reduced to /ən/ when it occurs between two subjects, objects, modifiers, verbs, or phrases.

They have long arms **and** legs. /ən/

She laughed **and** cried when she heard the news. /ən/

We stayed out late **and** went dancing. /ən/

BE CAREFUL! The vowel sound /æ/ in <u>and</u> is generally not reduced when it occurs at the beginning of a clause, but the consonant sound /d/ may still be dropped.

He wore a black suit, **and** she wore a green dress. /æn/

The initial /h/ sound is usually dropped in function words.

What does ̶h̶e mean? /dʌzi/

It's in ̶h̶is bag. /ɪnɪz/

A 🎧 Listen and practice.

1. I'll be going to the airport after dinner.
2. It's ten to two.
3. Look at that.
4. I got an iguana.
5. That's more than I need.
6. Pets are no trouble.
7. Is it black or white?
8. Where's your farm?
9. He's been gone for days.
10. They have long arms and legs.
11. She laughed and cried when she heard the news.
12. We stayed out late and went dancing.
13. He wore a black suit, and she wore a green dress.
14. What does he mean?
15. It's in his bag.

B Circle the words in the following sentences you think will be reduced.

1. Alternatives can be found for medical research on animals.
2. A lot can be done to improve conditions on those farms.
3. Animals are trained to perform in circuses.
4. Do animals have to be killed for their hides and fur?

🎧 Now practice reading each sentence aloud and listen to check.*

Unit 7

Vowel sounds /i/ and /ɪ/

The sound /i/ is longer and is formed by tensing the tongue.
The sound /ɪ/ is shorter and formed with the tongue relaxed.

/i/	/ɪ/
leave	live
team	Tim
feel	fill
steal	still
feet	fit

The vowel sound /ɪ/ also appears frequently in unstressed syllables.

places   market   artisan   minute   women

The vowel sounds /i/ and /ɪ/ are represented in spelling in a number of ways.

/i/	/ɪ/
steal	blimp
steep	syllable
people	busy
handy	building
believe	women
receive	pretty
boutique	been
key	give

A   Listen and practice.

1. leave   live
2. team   Tim
3. feel   fill
4. steal   still
5. feet   fit

B   Listen and practice.

1. places   **2.** market   **3.** artisan   **4.** minute   **5.** women

C   Listen to each pair of words. Circle if they are the <u>same</u> or <u>different</u>.

1. same   different   5. same   different
2. same   different   6. same   different
3. same   different   7. same   different
4. same   different   8. same   different

D   Listen and check which sound you hear.

	/i/	/ɪ/			/i/	/ɪ/			/i/	/ɪ/
1.	☐	☐		6.	☐	☐		11.	☐	☐
2.	☐	☐		7.	☐	☐		12.	☐	☐
3.	☐	☐		8.	☐	☐		13.	☐	☐
4.	☐	☐		9.	☐	☐		14.	☐	☐
5.	☐	☐		10.	☐	☐		15.	☐	☐

 Now listen again and practice.

Stress placement: prefixes and suffixes

Stress placement does not change when most prefixes and suffixes are added to a word.

important   unimportant   importance   importantly

obedient   obedience   disobedience   obediently

happy   unhappy   happiness   happily

However, adding the suffixes -<u>ion</u>, -<u>ic</u>, -<u>ity</u>, -<u>ical</u>, and -<u>ian</u> generally shifts stress to the syllable before the suffix.

educate   →   education

photograph   →   photographic

dependable   →   dependability

politics   →   political

music   →   musician

Some nouns and verbs have the same spelling. When the word is a noun, the stress is on the first syllable. When the word is a verb the stress is on the second syllable.

nouns	verbs
rebel	rebel
protest	protest
present	present
object	object
progress	progress

Other words in this category
conduct
conflict
contrast
convert
permit
record
survey
suspect

A 🎧 Listen and practice.

1. important   unimportant   importance   importantly
2. obedient   obedience   disobedience   obediently
3. happy   unhappy   happiness   happily

B 🎧 Listen and practice.

1. educate   education
2. photograph   photographic
3. dependable   dependability
4. politics   political
5. music   musician

C Look at the stressed syllable of each word in Column A. According to the rules given in the chart on page P7, mark the stressed syllable of each word in Column B.

	A	B
1.	fa mil iar	fa mil iar i ty
2.	e mo tion al	e mo tion al ly
3.	reg u late	reg u la tion
4.	ap pre ci a tive	ap pre cia tive ly
5.	sym pa thy	sym pa thet ic
6.	hy poth e size	hy po thet i cal
7.	beau ty	beau ti fy
8.	his to ry	his tor i cal
9.	ma te ri al ist	ma te ri al is tic
10.	pol i tics	pol i ti cian

⌒ Now practice reading each word aloud and listen to check.*

D ⌒ Listen and practice.

	nouns	**verbs**
1.	rebel	rebel
2.	protest	protest
3.	present	present
4.	object	object
5.	progress	progress

E Circle the syllable you think will be stressed in each blue word.

1. A summer fishing **permit permits** you to fish all you want.
2. The **protest** was organized to **protest** government spending.
3. All the employees were **surveyed** so the results of the **survey** would be useful.
4. The **contrast** between them now is not great compared to how much they **contrast** at other times of the year.
5. We strongly **object** to the decision to sell art **objects** outside the museum.

⌒ Now practice reading each sentence aloud, paying attention to words that are both nouns and verbs. Listen to check.*

Unit 9

Reduction and linking in perfect modals in the passive voice

In perfect modals in the passive voice, the modal and the auxiliary verbs <u>have been</u> are said together as one unit. Note that stress falls on the modal and the main verb. In everyday speech, the /h/ sound in the auxilliary <u>have</u> is dropped and /æ/ is reduced to /ə/.

/ˈkʊdəvbɪn/
They **COULD have been KILLED**.

/ˈmaɪtəvbɪn/
They **MIGHT have been LOST**.

/ˈməstəvbɪn/
They **MUST have been MOVED**.

/ˈmeɪyəvbɪn/
They **MAY have been DISCOVERED**.

With <u>had to</u>, stress <u>had</u> and the main verb. Say <u>had to</u> and <u>have been</u> as one unit.

/ˈhætuəvbɪn/
They **HAD to have been STOLEN**.

In negative perfect modals, stress falls on the modal, the word <u>not</u>, and the main verb. In everyday speech, <u>not</u> and the auxiliary verbs <u>have been</u> are generally said as one unit.

/ˈnatəvbɪn/
They **MIGHT NOT have been LOST**.
They **MUST NOT have been MOVED**.

A 🎧 Listen and practice.

1. They could have been killed.
2. They might have been lost.
3. They must have been moved.
4. They may have been discovered.
5. They had to have been stolen.
6. They might not have been lost.
7. They must not have been moved.

B Underline where you think the words should be linked and which sounds should be reduced.

1. The dinosaurs may have been killed by a meteor.
2. The trees could have been destroyed by a fire.
3. The gold figures may not have been lost.
4. The stone balls must have been moved using animals.
5. The drawings must not have been discovered until later.
6. The crater had to have been caused by a meteorite.
7. The trees couldn't have been burned in a fire.

🎧 Now practice reading each sentence aloud, paying attention to reductions. Listen to check.*

Unit 10

Vowel sounds /eɪ/, /ɛ/, /æ/, and /ʌ/

The sound /eɪ/ is longer and is formed by tensing the tongue with the lips spread.
The sounds /ɛ/, /æ/, and /ʌ/ are shorter and are formed with the tongue relaxed.
Say /eɪ/ and /ɛ/ with the lips spread wide. Say /æ/ with the lips spread slightly and the
mouth slightly open. Say /ʌ/ with the tongue and jaw completely relaxed.

Mouth positions for vowels	
tongue tensed (long)	/eɪ/
tongue relaxed (short)	/ɛ/, /æ/, /ʌ/
lips spread	/eɪ/, /ɛ/, /æ/
jaw relaxed	/ʌ/

/eɪ/	/ɛ/	/æ/	/ʌ/
pain	pen	pan	pun
Dane	den	Dan	done
mate	met	mat	mutt
bait	bet	bat	but

The vowel sounds /eɪ/, /ɛ/, /æ/, and /ʌ/ may
be represented by these spellings.

/eɪ/	/ɛ/	/æ/	/ʌ/
pay	get	catch	jumping
weigh	sweat	have	nothing
shape	says	laugh	touch
wait	said	half	does
table	friend	guarantee	blood
great	guest	relax	what

A 🎧 Listen and practice.

1. pain	pen	pan	pun
2. Dane	den	Dan	done
3. mate	met	mat	mutt
4. bait	bet	bat	but

B 🎧 Listen to each word and place it in the correct column.

edge   games   enough   can't   bungee   rafting   nothing   chance   sweat   wait   scare

/eɪ/	/ɛ/	/æ/	/ʌ/
....	....	....	....
....	....	....	....
....	....	....	....
....	....	....	....

🎧 Now practice reading each word aloud and listen again to check.*

C 🎧 Listen to each sentence and circle the word you hear.

1. Give the money to the (men / man).
2. I think it's (Dan / done).
3. What is that (rag / rug) made of?
4. Do you need this (pen / pan)?
5. He's a perfect (mutt / mate).
6. My (date / debt) is causing me trouble.
7. Could you take that (bug / bag) off the counter?
8. Please put a bandage on the (cut / cat).

Now practice reading the sentences both ways.